ADVANTAGE Test Prep 6

Table of Contents

Introduction 3

Reading

Introduction to Reading 6
Nonfiction Reading Selection: *Just a Jungle?* 7

Vocabulary
Multimeaning Words 8
Analogies 9

Comprehension
Implied Main Idea 10
Make Generalizations 11
Sequence 12
Compare and Contrast 13
Fiction Reading Selection: *The Tree Huggers* 14
Characterization 15
Predict Outcomes 16
Draw Conclusions 17
Symbolism 18
Summarize 19
Poetry Reading Selection: "Gathering Leaves" 20
Point of View 21
Setting 22
Cause and Effect 23
Extend Meaning 24

Graphic Information
Map Reading 25
Diagrams 26
Charts and Graphs 27

Reference Sources
Using a Glossary 28
Dictionary Entry 29

Writing

Introduction to Writing: Understanding Writing Prompts 30
Understanding Scoring Rubrics .. 31
Brainstorming and Organizing your Ideas 32
Writing Prompt and Writer's Checklist 33
Plan and Write Your First Draft ... 34
Write Your Final Draft 36
Give Yourself a Score 38

Language

Introduction to Language 39

Mechanics
Capitalization and End Marks 40
Quotation Marks 41
Commas and Semicolons 42
Apostrophes 43

Grammar and Usage
Nouns 44
Pronouns 45
Regular and Irregular Verbs 46
Verb Tenses 47
Adjectives 48
Adverbs 49
Comparatives 50
Conjunctions 51
Modifiers 52

Table of Contents

Prepositions 53
Sentence Formation 54
Spelling
Easily Confused Words 55
Compound Words 56

Introduction to Math 57
Number Sense and Numeration
Read and Write Whole Numbers and
    Decimals in Expanded Form . . 58
Compare and Order Fractions,
    Decimals, and Percents 59
Exponential Notation 60
Computation and Operations
Add and Subtract Fractions and
    Mixed Numbers 61
Add and Subtract Positive and
    Negative Numbers 62
Multiply and Divide Decimals 63
Multiply and Divide Fractions and
    Mixed Numbers 64
Multiply and Divide Positive and
    Negative Numbers 65
Order of Operations 66
Estimation and Number Theory
Estimate to Predict Results 67
Greatest Common Factor 68
Least Common Multiple 69

Prime Factorization 70
Measurement
Circumference 71
Classify Triangles 72
Sum of the Angles of a Triangle . . 73
Length, Weight, and Capacity 74
Geometry
Congruent and Similar Figures . . . 75
Algebraic Thinking, Data Analysis, Probability
Use Variables 76
Equations and Inequalities 77
Problem Solving
Solve One-Step and Two-Step
    Problems 78
Estimate Solutions 79
Apply Geometric Properties 80

Practice Test Introduction 81
Student Information Sheet 82
Answer Sheet 83
Practice Test: Reading 84
Practice Test: Writing 90
Practice Test: Language 96
Practice Test: Math 102

Answer Key 108

CREDITS
Concept Development: Kent Publishing Services, Inc.
Written by: Linda Barr and Randy Green
Editor: Carla Hamaguchi
Designer/Production: Moonhee Pak/Mary Gagné
Illustrators: Frank Ordaz and Corbin Hillam
Art Director: Tom Cochrane
Project Director: Carolea Williams

© 2004 Creative Teaching Press, Inc., Huntington Beach, CA 92649
Reproduction of activities in any manner for use in the classroom and not for commercial sale is permissible.
Reproduction of these materials for an entire school or for a school system is strictly prohibited.

Introduction

Testing is a big part of education today, and this workbook is designed to help students become better prepared to succeed at taking standardized and proficiency tests. This workbook contains skills and strategies that can be used in any kind of testing situation. Even if students don't have to take standardized tests, they will still benefit from studying the skills and strategies in this workbook.

Standardized Tests
Standardized tests get their name because they are administered in the exact same way to hundreds of thousands of students across the country. They are also referred to as *norm-referenced tests.* Norms give educators a common standard of measurement of students' skills and abilities across the country. Students are ranked according to their test scores and then assigned a percentile ranking. This ranking tells what percent of all students scored better or worse than the norm.

Proficiency Tests
Many states develop their own statewide proficiency tests. Proficiency tests are also known as *criterion-referenced tests.* This means that the test is based on a list of standards and skills (criteria). States develop standards for what students should know at each grade level. The proficiency test evaluates how well students have mastered these standards.

Although both tests may look similar, they measure different things. A proficiency test measures a student's mastery of set standards. A standardized test compares a student's achievement to others who took the same test across the country.

Many tests were reviewed in developing the material for this workbook. They include the following:
- **California Achievement Tests (CAT)**
- **Comprehensive Tests of Basic Skills (CTBS)**
- **TerraNova**
- **Iowa Tests of Basic Skills (ITBS)**
- **Metropolitan Achievement Tests (MAT)**
- **Stanford Achievement Tests (SAT)**
- **Texas Assessment of Knowledge and Skills (TAKS)**

It is important to recognize that all national standardized achievement tests work essentially the same way. They ask multiple-choice questions, have specific time limits, and compare your child's results to national averages. The goal of this test-prep series is to teach **test-taking strategies** so that no matter which test your child is required to take, he or she will be successful.

Introduction

Preparing for Tests

The more students are prepared for taking standardized and proficiency tests, the better they will do on those tests. A student who understands the skills commonly measured and who practices test-taking strategies will be more likely to be a successful test-taker. The more the student knows and knows what to expect, the more comfortable he or she will be in actual test-taking situations.

Standardized and proficiency testing is used to:
- evaluate students' progress, strengths, and weaknesses.
- show how each student's school achievement compares with other students on a local and nationwide level (standardized).
- show an individual student's achievement of set standards (proficiency).
- select students for remedial or achievement programs.
- tell educators whether school systems are succeeding.
- evaluate the success of school programs.
- help educators develop programs to suit their students' specific needs.

Standardized tests are only one measure of student achievement, however. Teachers use many other methods to gain insights into each student's skills, abilities, and knowledge. They evaluate students through day-to-day observation, evaluation, and assessment.

Introduction

How Can Parents Help Children Succeed at Standardized Testing?

The following list includes suggestions on how to prepare your child for testing.

Tips for Parents
- Monitor your child's progress.
- Get to know your child's teacher, and find out what he or she thinks you can do to help your child at home.
- Be informed about your state's testing requirements.
- Motivate your child to prepare.
- Make homework part of your child's daily routine.
- Set aside a period of time each day to study with your child.
- Read aloud to your child.
- Share learning experiences with your child.
- Make sure your child is getting the sleep and nutrition he or she needs to succeed.
- Always nurture your child's curiosity and desire to learn.
- Encourage your child to learn about computers and technology.
- Encourage your child to take tests very seriously but to have healthy expectations and keep testing in perspective.
- Offer encouragement and support so that your child wants to make a good effort.

Where Can I Learn More About Testing?

ERIC Clearinghouse on Assessment and Evaluation
209 O'Boyle Hall
The Catholic University of America
Washington, DC 20064
(202) 319-5120
http://ericae.net/

National Center for Fair and Open Testing, Inc. (FairTest)
342 Broadway
Cambridge, MA 02139
http://www.fairtest.org/

Introduction to Reading

Reading is a skill that will help you do well in school and in life—and on standardized and proficiency tests. The more you read, the better you will read. The better you read, the more you will enjoy it, and the higher you will score on tests. Read often, and experiment with many different types of reading materials. Read alone and with others. Read aloud sometimes. Practice listening to how words sound. As you read, think about how stories develop and progress.

Nearly every standardized or proficiency test includes a section on reading. The reading passages may be fiction, nonfiction, or poetry. They may also include graphic information, such as maps, or reference information, such as glossaries and dictionaries. You will be asked to recall, interpret, and reflect on what you read.

The following pages will help you review reading skills. You will practice the skills with questions similar to the ones on standardized tests. If you practice these skills now, you'll perform better on tests. In this workbook section, you will learn to:

- find words that have the **same or similar meaning.**
- find words that have **opposite meanings.**
- solve problems that involve **analogies.**
- recognize details that **compare or contrast.**
- understand the **main idea** of a passage.
- identify **details** and understand how they support the main idea.
- see the connection between **cause and effect.**
- **predict outcomes** based on what you read.
- **draw conclusions** and support them with evidence.
- determine the author's **point of view** and how it affects a story.
- analyze the **setting** of a story or poem.
- know the **characters** in a story.
- **make generalizations** about what you read.
- **extend meaning** by understanding more than what the author said.
- see the **sequence of events,** the order in which things happen.
- understand **graphic information** in maps, graphs, charts, schedules, and diagrams.
- use **reference sources** such as library materials, indexes, and tables of contents.

Read the passage and then complete the activities on pages 8 through 13.

Just a Jungle?

Some people think that *jungle* is another name for a rain forest. However, *jungle* is the correct term for the thick, scrubby vegetation that grows after a true rain forest has been destroyed. A jungle is much better than a bare patch of land, but we need to protect the true rain forests so they do not become jungles.

Located near the equator, tropical rain forests cover only about six percent of Earth's surface. Still, these forests are home to more than half of the plant and animal species on Earth, roughly 30 million of them. Scientists have not even identified all of these species yet.

You might wonder why it's important to identify all these species. One important reason is that about 7,000 of the medicines we use today came from plants. Many of these plants first grew in rain forests. For example, medical treatments for hypertension (high blood pressure) and rheumatoid arthritis (stiff joints) came from rain forest plants.

So far, scientists have had time to test less than one percent of the plants in the rain forests to see if they can be used as medicine. Our best chance of curing cancer and AIDS might be growing deep in a forest right now. However, an area of rain forest as big as Wyoming is destroyed every year. More than 100 species disappear from the rain forests every day, which could mean that a cure for cancer might be gone by next week.

Why would anyone destroy the rain forests? People who live in and near the rain forests cut or burn trees to clear land for farming and grazing. However, rain forest soil has few nutrients in it. The soil needs a steady supply of dead leaves falling from many plants to enrich it. After a year or two, crops do not grow well in this poor soil. The farmers abandon the fields, letting rain and wind blow much of the soil away. Then they clear more land for their crops.

Valuable trees grow in the rain forests. They are cut down and used to make expensive furniture and ornaments. Logging companies make huge profits from selling this wood. The people living in the forests support their families by helping with the logging.

Too much of the rain forests is already gone. To protect the rest of the forests, we must find ways to use them without destroying them. Many organizations are doing that right now. You can use the Internet to find information about these groups and find out how you can help. Learning about the rain forests is your first step in helping to save them!

VOCABULARY

KNOW THE SKILL: **MULTIMEANING WORDS**

Some words can have several different meanings. For example, the word *rare* can describe meat that is barely cooked, or it can describe something that is hard to find. When you encounter a multimeaning word, the rest of the sentence or paragraph will tell you which meaning is being used.

DURING THE TEST

When answering a test question about a word with several meanings, reread the rest of the sentence or paragraph. Look for clues that tell you which meaning is being used in that sentence.

TEST EXAMPLE

1. The passage says that a jungle is better than a bare *patch* of land. What does the word *patch* mean here?
    - Ⓐ to mend a hole
    - Ⓑ a separate area
    - Ⓒ a small piece of cloth
    - Ⓓ a temporary connection

THINK ABOUT THE ANSWER

The answer is B. This sentence refers to an area of land. Options A, C, and D are other definitions of *patch*, but they do not make sense in this sentence.

NOW YOU TRY IT

2. The last paragraph talks about protecting the *rest* of the forests. What does the word *rest* mean in this sentence?
    - Ⓕ to lean something against a wall
    - Ⓖ to lie or sit quietly
    - Ⓗ to be motionless
    - Ⓙ the remainder

Check your answer on page 108.

"Overview" the Test

If you are allowed, quickly flip through the pages of the test so that you will know what lies ahead. This will help you plan your time. If you are permitted to write on the test, jot notes to yourself. Quickly judge how much time you will need for each part.

VOCABULARY

KNOW THE SKILL: ANALOGIES

An analogy is a word problem. Here is an example: *Green* is to *grass* as *blue* is to ____. You must supply a word to complete the sentence. To do that, you must figure out the relationship between the first two words. In this case, the first word describes the color of the second word. *Green* is the color of *grass,* and *blue* is the color of—the *sky.* The pairs of words might also be synonyms or antonyms or have another relationship to each other.

DURING THE TEST

Begin by determining the relationship between the first two words. For example, the first word might be an example of the second word, as in: *Dog* is to *animal* as *ant* is to ____. Then see which word choice has the same relationship to the third word. (A good choice would be *insect.*)

TEST EXAMPLE

1. *Tree* is to *forest* as *snowflake* is to _____.
   - Ⓐ frozen water
   - Ⓑ avalanche
   - Ⓒ raindrop
   - Ⓓ leaves

THINK ABOUT THE ANSWER

The answer is B, *avalanche.* A tree is part of a forest, like a snowflake is part of an avalanche. A snowflake is made of frozen water, but a tree is not made of a forest (option A). A snowflake is a frozen raindrop, but a tree is not a frozen forest (option C). Leaves are part of a tree, but they are not part of a snowflake (option D).

NOW YOU TRY IT

2. *Support* is to *neglect* as *expensive* is to _____.
   - Ⓕ cheap
   - Ⓖ costly
   - Ⓗ dollars
   - Ⓙ valuable

Check your answer on page 108.

Keep Learning New Words

Continually expand your vocabulary. You can do this by reading books, magazines, and newspapers. You can use your fabulous vocabulary to provide vivid and interesting test answers.

COMPREHENSION

KNOW THE SKILL: IMPLIED MAIN IDEA

Every reading passage has a main idea, although it may not be stated. When something is not expressed directly it is said to be *implied*. The main idea is the author's most important point, which is then clarified by details in the passage.

DURING THE TEST

As you read, note the details, but watch for the most important idea, the point that the details tell about. To determine the main idea, ask yourself, "What does this author want me to remember?"

TEST EXAMPLE

1. Which is the unstated (implied) main idea of the first paragraph of this passage?
   - Ⓐ What grows after a rain forest is destroyed is called a jungle.
   - Ⓑ Rain forests are more valuable than jungles.
   - Ⓒ Rain forests are sometimes called jungles.
   - Ⓓ Jungles are thick, scrubby vegetation.

THINK ABOUT THE ANSWER

The answer is B. It is implied by the sentence "…we need to protect the true rain forests so they do not become jungles." Options A, C, and D are true, but they are details that support the main idea.

NOW YOU TRY IT

2. Write two or more sentences that explain the main idea of the entire passage.

_____
_____
_____

Check your answer on page 108.

Have a Plan
Have a plan for answering every type of question. Know what to expect from questions so that you know to consider everything that is important. Some people like to answer easy questions within a section first because it might help them answer the harder questions later.

10   *Advantage Test Prep Grade 6* © 2004 Creative Teaching Press

COMPREHENSION

KNOW THE SKILL: MAKE GENERALIZATIONS

When you make generalizations, first you draw a conclusion based on what you have read and what you already know. Then you use this conclusion to make a generalization: if this is true, then that is true, too. You go beyond what you have read and know, but not too far beyond. If you go too far beyond, your generalization will probably not be true.

DURING THE TEST

First, eliminate the answer choices that don't seem likely or possible. Then consider each of the remaining choices. Make sure the information in the passage supports your answer choice.

TEST EXAMPLE

1. The people living in the rain forest probably
   - Ⓐ are excellent farmers.
   - Ⓑ do not value the plants of the rain forest.
   - Ⓒ do not realize that the plants can be used as medicine.
   - Ⓓ have to balance protecting the forest with supporting their families.

THINK ABOUT THE ANSWER

Option D is the answer. The passage suggests that these people struggle as farmers (option A). However, we can conclude that they value the plants that grow in the rain forest (option B) and use many of them as food and medicine (option C).

NOW YOU TRY IT

2. Which generalization is probably the most accurate?
   - Ⓕ Plants are the most important source of medicine.
   - Ⓖ The rain forests contain many unknown treasures.
   - Ⓗ The rain forests will survive, no matter what people do to them.
   - Ⓙ The people who live in the rain forests are the biggest threat to them.

Check your answer on page 108.

Learn from Every Test
Every test you take is preparation for the next test. After completing a test, write in your journal what challenged you and how you could have been more prepared. List all the spelling words you can remember from the test, and memorize them.

Advantage Test Prep Grade 6 © 2004 Creative Teaching Press

COMPREHENSION

KNOW THE SKILL: SEQUENCE

Sequence is the chronological order of events in a passage, the order in which things happen. Paying attention to this order helps you better understand the passage.

DURING THE TEST

As you read a passage, notice the order in which events are described. You might find some signal words to help indicate sequence, such as *first, then, before, after, next,* and *finally.*

TEST EXAMPLE

1. What happens after crops grow for a year or two in an area of a rain forest?
   - Ⓐ The farmers cut or burn the trees on this land.
   - Ⓑ The crops take most of the nutrients out of the soil.
   - Ⓒ The crops add many nutrients to the soil.
   - Ⓓ Rain and wind soon blow the soil away.

THINK ABOUT THE ANSWER

Option B is the answer. Option A happens before the crops are planted. Option C does not happen. Option D happens after the nutrients are gone from the soil and the farmers abandon the fields.

NOW YOU TRY IT

2. Which of these events happens last?
   - Ⓕ The plant turns out to be a valuable medicine.
   - Ⓖ A new species of plant is found in the rain forest.
   - Ⓗ This new medicine helps us stay well or get well.
   - Ⓙ Scientists test the new species to see how it affects human diseases.

Check your answer on page 108.

Plan Your Time

Plan your time, and do not linger on a section if you are done with it. Move on to the next section. Work quickly, but not so quickly that you make mistakes.

COMPREHENSION

KNOW THE SKILL: **COMPARE AND CONTRAST**

Sometimes authors help readers visualize a scene or understand an idea by comparing it with something that the readers already know. Other times, authors describe something by contrasting it, that is, explaining how the two things are different.

DURING THE TEST

A question might ask you how two things are the same, how they are different, or both. Read the passage again. Look for explanations of how things are the same or different. Words and phrases such as *like*, *same as*, *similar*, and *also* indicate that things are being compared. Words and phrases such as *on the other hand* and *however* indicate that things are being contrasted.

TEST EXAMPLE

1. Write two or more sentences to explain two ways that tropical rain forests are different from other types of forests.

   _____
   _____
   _____

THINK ABOUT THE ANSWER

Your answer might have made these points: Rain forests have more species of plants and animals than other forests. Rain forests were named because they get more rain than other forests.

NOW YOU TRY IT

2. Write two or more sentences to explain two ways that tropical rain forests are the same as other forests.

   _____
   _____
   _____

Check your answer on page 108.

Review Your Work

If you finish the test before time is up, don't leave! Use every minute that is left to check your work. Quickly make sure that you have answered all the questions. Check your answer sheet for mistakes. Proofread any writing. Double-check the placement of decimal points and commas in numbers.

Advantage Test Prep Grade 6 © 2004 Creative Teaching Press

Read *The Tree Huggers*, based on a folktale from India. Then complete the activities on pages 15 through 19.

THE TREE HUGGERS

Amrita was a young girl who lived in a small village in India long ago, when the maharajahs ruled. She loved the trees that grew in a circle around the village and had a favorite one that she hugged every day. This tall tree shaded her from the burning desert sun and protected her from howling sandstorms.

One day Amrita spotted soldiers carrying axes. "What are you going to do?" she asked fearfully.

The leader frowned at her. "The Maharajah needs wood to build his new fortress!"

Soon the men started chopping down the trees, including the one Amrita hugged every day. She begged them to stop, but they kept chopping until her beloved tree crashed to the ground. She hurried to hug another one so it would not be hurt, too. When the villagers heard the falling trees and saw what Amrita was doing, they hurried to hug other trees. The leader shouted at the villagers to go away, but they refused to move. Finally, the soldiers gave up. "The Maharajah will be very angry with you people," the leader warned them as he and his men left.

"What is going to happen to the trees?" the villagers asked Amrita.

"I don't know," she answered, "but we must be ready to protect them."

The next day, the Maharajah himself rode to the village, sitting stiffly on his tall horse. When he saw the villagers still hugging the trees, he shouted, "How dare you disobey me!"

The villagers were too frightened to say anything, but finally Amrita stepped forward. "Great Sir, we need these trees to protect our village."

"Well, I need these trees to build my fortress." Then the Maharajah turned to his men. "Cut down these trees and be quick about it," he ordered.

But as soon as the soldiers stepped toward the villagers and the trees, a huge sandstorm roared toward them. As the wind drove the sand into their faces, the soldiers joined the villagers huddled under the trees. Even the Maharajah and his stallion took shelter there. After the storm had passed, broken branches lay everywhere, but the trees had protected the huts in the village.

The Maharajah silently surveyed the damage. "Villagers, you have shown great courage to protect your trees. You are also very wise, as these trees protect you in return. I hereby order that these trees will never be cut. We will find wood for the fortress someplace else."

The villagers rejoiced and marked the place where Amrita's favorite tree had stood so no one would forget it. Every day after that, Amrita still went into the forest and hugged the trees. "How can we live without you?" she asked.

COMPREHENSION

KNOW THE SKILL: CHARACTERIZATION

Authors show what the characters are like through their words, thoughts, and actions. You can also learn about characters from the author's descriptions of them and the way that other characters react to them.

DURING THE TEST

Test questions may ask you to describe a character, so pay attention to descriptive words. Also notice what characters do, say, and think and how they interact with other characters.

TEST EXAMPLE

 Which word BEST describes Amrita?
- Ⓐ fierce
- Ⓑ fearful
- Ⓒ careless
- Ⓓ thoughtful

THINK ABOUT THE ANSWER

Option D is correct. Amrita loves the trees because she realizes that they protect her. Nothing in the passage suggests that she is fierce (option A) or careless (option C). She is the only villager brave enough to talk to the Maharajah, so we would not describe her as fearful (option B).

NOW YOU TRY IT

 How can you tell that the villagers respect Amrita?
- Ⓕ They know she hugs trees.
- Ⓖ They hurry to try to save the trees.
- Ⓗ They ask her what will happen next.
- Ⓙ They celebrate after the Maharajah leaves.

Check your answer on page 108.

Watch for Certain Words

Keep an eye out for words like *not*, *but*, *best*, and *except*. These words place limits on the answer. Also watch out for absolute words like *always*, *never*, and *only*. One of these words in a question means there can be no exceptions.

COMPREHENSION

KNOW THE SKILL: PREDICT OUTCOMES

When you know what has happened so far in a story and you know how people usually act, you can often predict what will happen next. In a test, you might also be asked to predict what will happen after the story ends.

DURING THE TEST

As you read, try to predict what the characters will do next. Then you can see if your predictions were correct. If you were mistaken, identify the clues you missed. This will help you learn from the situation.

TEST EXAMPLE

1. Write two or more sentences to describe what Amrita will be like when she is an adult. What will she care about? How will others treat her? Provide reasons for your predictions, based on the story and your own experience.
_____
_____
_____

THINK ABOUT THE ANSWER

Did you write that Amrita will continue to care about trees and other living things when she is older because she cares so strongly about them now? Perhaps you are the same way or know others who are. The villagers might choose Amrita as their leader because they ask her for guidance even now when she is young. Amrita will take good care of the village because she is brave and wise beyond her years.

NOW YOU TRY IT

2. After this experience with Amrita and the villagers, where will this Maharajah tell the soldiers to gather wood for his new fortress? Give reasons for your prediction, based on the story and your own experience.

Check your answer on page 108.
_____
_____
_____

Stay Focused
Do not let anything distract you, especially other test-takers. Don't waste time looking out the window or at other people in the room. You should have only one focus—the test!

COMPREHENSION

KNOW THE SKILL: DRAW CONCLUSIONS

When you draw a conclusion, you figure out something about a story, an event, or a character that the author did not directly tell you. To draw a conclusion, you use information from the passage, plus your own experience.

DURING THE TEST

As you read, think about why characters do certain things and why certain events take place. Don't just read the words: think about the reasons behind what is happening.

TEST EXAMPLE

1. What motivated Amrita to step forward and confront the Maharajah?
   - Ⓐ She wanted to show how brave she was.
   - Ⓑ She thought he was not a good ruler.
   - Ⓒ She was young and disrespectful.
   - Ⓓ She wanted to protect the trees.

THINK ABOUT THE ANSWER

Option D is the answer. Amrita might not have been brave all the time, but her love for the trees made her brave (option A). The passage does not tell us what she thought of the Maharajah (option B). Calling the ruler "Great Sir" shows that she was respectful (option C).

NOW YOU TRY IT

2. Why did the Maharajah order his soldiers to cut down the trees?
   - Ⓕ He cared only about his own needs.
   - Ⓖ He did not care if a sandstorm ruined the village.
   - Ⓗ He did not realize how strong sandstorms could be.
   - Ⓙ He wanted to show the villagers who was in charge.

Check your answer on page 108.

Don't Get Stuck!
Sometimes you'll come across a tricky question, but don't let it worry you. Reread the question, then try to solve it. If you are stumped, circle the question and move on. You can come back to it later. If you still don't know the answer, make your best guess.

Advantage Test Prep Grade 6 © 2004 Creative Teaching Press

COMPREHENSION

KNOW THE SKILL: SYMBOLISM

A *symbol* is a person, place, event, or object that has a special meaning. For example, the American flag is a symbol of our nation. In a certain story, an apple might be a symbol of sharing. Not every reading passage contains a symbol, but many do. You are very likely to be asked about symbolism in tests.

DURING THE TEST

As you read, look for ideas or objects that are repeated. Think about whether these ideas or objects have a deeper meaning. Perhaps the author is using them as a symbol of something.

TEST EXAMPLE

1. In *The Tree Huggers*, what might the sandstorm symbolize?
    - Ⓐ nature's power
    - Ⓑ a threat to the village
    - Ⓒ the Maharajah's power
    - Ⓓ the determination of the villagers

THINK ABOUT THE ANSWER

Option A is the answer. Although the storm is a threat to the village, this threat is based on facts, not a use of symbolism (option B). The storm is not under the control of the Maharajah (option C) or the villagers (option D).

NOW YOU TRY IT

2. What do the trees symbolize for Amrita?
    - Ⓕ the problems we face in life
    - Ⓖ safety and protection
    - Ⓗ shade from the sun
    - Ⓙ independence

Check your answer on page 108.

Don't Waste Time

Don't waste time memorizing details from reading passages. Scan the questions to find out what you need to know, and then answer the questions with the information you have. You usually do not need all the information in a reading passage to answer the questions.

COMPREHENSION

KNOW THE SKILL: SUMMARIZE

To summarize, you explain the most important ideas and facts in a passage, leaving out details. A summary may be one sentence or several, depending on the length of the passage.

DURING THE TEST

As you read, look for main ideas that would be included in a summary. If you know you will be asked to write a summary, underline or jot down these main ideas.

TEST EXAMPLE

1. The first three paragraphs of this passage end with the soldiers leaving to report to the Maharajah. What is the best summary of these three paragraphs?

   Ⓐ Amrita lived in a small village that was ruled by a Maharajah.
   Ⓑ Amrita and the villagers stopped soldiers from cutting down trees.
   Ⓒ Soldiers cut down Amrita's favorite tree, and she was heartbroken.
   Ⓓ The Maharajah's soldiers were angry with Amrita and the other villagers.

THINK ABOUT THE ANSWER

Option B is the answer. Options A, C, and D are details from the paragraphs. They do not summarize the important points.

NOW YOU TRY IT

2. What is the best summary of the entire story?
   Ⓕ Amrita and a sandstorm saved the trees that protected her village.
   Ⓖ The Maharajah learned an important lesson about his people.
   Ⓗ Amrita showed how brave she could be in the face of danger.
   Ⓙ The power of nature is greater than any human ruler.

Check your answer on page 108.

Don't Panic!
If you are getting anxious before or during the test, take several slow, deep breaths to relax. Visualize being in a peaceful and calm place. Remind yourself that you are well prepared. Don't talk to other students before the test because anxiety can be contagious!

Advantage Test Prep Grade 6 © 2004 Creative Teaching Press

Gathering Leaves

BY ROBERT FROST

Spades take up leaves
No better than spoons,
And bags full of leaves
Are light as balloons.

I make a great noise
Of rustling all day
Like rabbit and deer
Running away.

But the mountains I raise
Elude my embrace,
Flowing over my arms
And into my face.

I may load and unload
Again and again
Till I fill the whole shed,
And what have I then?

Next to nothing for weight,
And since they grew duller
From contact with earth,
Next to nothing for color.

Next to nothing for use.
But a crop is a crop,
And who's to say where
The harvest shall stop?

COMPREHENSION

KNOW THE SKILL: POINT OF VIEW

A poem or story is told through the eyes of a certain person, from that person's point of view. The two points of view used most often are first person and third person. First person means that the narrator is a character in the story and uses the pronouns *I, me, my,* and so on. Readers learn only what this character learns. Third person means that the story is told by a narrator who is not a character in the story. The characters are referred to as *he* or *she* and so on. In this case, readers might learn what several different characters learn.

DURING THE TEST

As you read a passage, ask yourself who is speaking. Who is telling the story or describing the events? Through whose eyes do you see?

TEST EXAMPLE

1. From whose point of view is this poem told?
   - Ⓐ the leaves themselves
   - Ⓑ an animal scampering through the leaves
   - Ⓒ someone who is trying to rake up the leaves
   - Ⓓ someone who is watching another person rake the leaves

THINK ABOUT THE ANSWER

Option C is correct because one line says, "I may load and unload again and again." The leaves do not talk (option A), nor do the animals mentioned in the poem (option B). No other person is apparently in sight (option D).

NOW YOU TRY IT

2. Is this poem written in the first person or the third person? Give reasons for your answer.

_____

_____

_____

Check your answer on page 108.

Don't Rely on Your Memory
When answering questions about a reading passage, go back and skim the passage again. Then read the question, and carefully read the passage, looking for the answer.

Advantage Test Prep Grade 6 © 2004 Creative Teaching Press

COMPREHENSION

KNOW THE SKILL: SETTING

The setting is both the physical location of the action in a story and the time period when the story takes place. Some passages move through several settings. A setting can matter little or be very important. For example, a passage that takes place during the Revolutionary War might be greatly affected by the events of that time. This passage would also be influenced by whether it took place in England or Massachusetts.

DURING THE TEST

Ask yourself where and when the passage takes place. Then consider how the setting affects the passage. Would the passage change if it were set in a different place or time?

TEST EXAMPLE

1. What is the setting of this poem?
    - A. outside during autumn
    - B. inside during autumn
    - C. outside during spring
    - D. inside during spring

THINK ABOUT THE ANSWER

Option A is the answer. The narrator is gathering leaves that have fallen from the trees. Therefore, the setting is not inside (options B and D) or during spring (options C and D).

NOW YOU TRY IT

2. Could the setting of this poem be changed? Why or why not?

_____
_____
_____

Check your answer on page 108.

Use Your Favorite Pencil
If you have a favorite pencil, it can help you feel more comfortable when you take your test. It should have a good eraser to clean away any answers that you might want to change.

Comprehension

KNOW THE SKILL: CAUSE AND EFFECT

Some questions ask you to identify what caused something or what the effect of something was. A *cause* is the reason why something happens. An *effect* is the result of an event or an action.

DURING THE TEST

To find a cause as you read, ask yourself, "What caused this? Why did this happen?" To find an effect, ask yourself, "What results from this?"

TEST EXAMPLE

1. In the second stanza of the poem, what causes the rustling sound?
    - Ⓐ rabbit and deer walking in the leaves
    - Ⓑ rabbit and deer running away
    - Ⓒ jumping in the leaves
    - Ⓓ raking the leaves

THINK ABOUT THE ANSWER

Option D is the answer. The author makes this noise as he rakes. The sound is *like* rabbit and deer running away, but it is not caused by these animals (options A and B). The author does not mention jumping in the leaves (option C).

NOW YOU TRY IT

2. What was the result of the leaves lying on the ground?
    - Ⓕ They became lightweight.
    - Ⓖ They made rustling sounds.
    - Ⓗ They lost their bright colors.
    - Ⓙ They heaped up into mountains.

Check your answer on page 108.

Read the Directions Carefully
This is a no-brainer! Pay attention while you read the directions. It will help you avoid careless errors.

Advantage Test Prep Grade 6 © 2004 Creative Teaching Press

COMPREHENSION

KNOW THE SKILL: EXTEND MEANING

The message in a poem is often not stated in so many words. The author wants you to think about the meaning and apply it to your own life. For example, this poem describes gathering leaves, but it is really about more than this task.

DURING THE TEST

When a question asks you about something that is not directly stated in the passage, go beyond the meaning of the words in the passage. What is the author saying about life in general?

TEST EXAMPLE

1. The poem seems to be about raking leaves, but it is also about
   - Ⓐ cleaning up a yard.
   - Ⓑ doing what you were told to do.
   - Ⓒ making the most of a necessary task.
   - Ⓓ the wild animals that live in the forests.

THINK ABOUT THE ANSWER

Option C is correct because Frost hints that the task is endless and concludes with "next to nothing for use." However, it is necessary, so you might as well make the most of it because "a crop is a crop." Frost does not mention cleaning up a yard (option A) or being assigned the task (option B). Rabbit and deer are mentioned, but they are a detail, not the focus of the poem (option D).

NOW YOU TRY IT

2. The poem ends with this stanza: "Next to nothing for use. But a crop is a crop, and who's to say where the harvest shall stop?" What did Frost mean here?
   - Ⓕ Leaves are one kind of crop.
   - Ⓖ We don't know when we should stop raking.
   - Ⓗ Who knows how long it will take to rake all the leaves?
   - Ⓙ We really don't know what has value and what does not.

Check your answer on page 108.

Use the Process of Elimination

First, rule out any answers that you know are wrong. Then rule out answers that are partly wrong or don't seem to fit. If two options are very similar, they might both be incorrect. This process will help you narrow down possible answers.

Graphic Information

KNOW THE SKILL: MAP READING

On some tests, you may be asked to read a map. You might have to give or follow directions or identify places on the map. Skill in map reading will help you for your entire life.

DURING THE TEST

First, review the map and figure out what it shows. Find the compass rose and study it to determine direction and the scale for measuring distance. Notice the other features that are labeled.

TEST EXAMPLE

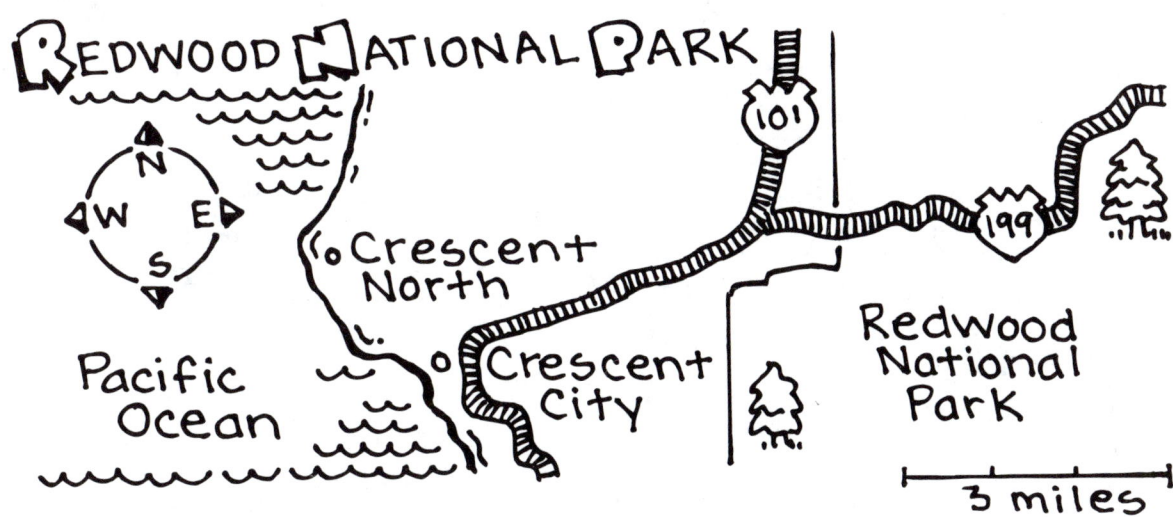

1 Study this map of the Redwood National Park in northern California. If you were in Crescent City, what direction would you drive on a major highway to get to the park?

- Ⓐ directly west
- Ⓑ directly south
- Ⓒ northeast
- Ⓓ northwest

THINK ABOUT THE ANSWER

Option C is correct. You would travel northeast on Highway 199 to get to the park. Options A and D both lead into the Pacific Ocean. Option B moves away from the park.

NOW YOU TRY IT

2 If you could drive from the closest edge of the park directly to Crescent City, about how far would you drive?

- Ⓕ 1 mile
- Ⓖ 3 miles
- Ⓗ 6 miles
- Ⓙ 9 miles

Check your answer on page 109.

Advantage Test Prep Grade 6 © 2004 Creative Teaching Press

Graphic Information

KNOW THE SKILL: DIAGRAMS

Diagrams can show the names of parts or show how something works. Diagrams often can explain something more clearly than paragraphs of words.

DURING THE TEST

When you see a diagram on a test, read the title and then read each label that names a part and perhaps explains what that part does. After reading the question, consider each answer, checking to see if it matches the information in the diagram. You should be able to rule out all but one option, the correct choice.

TEST EXAMPLE

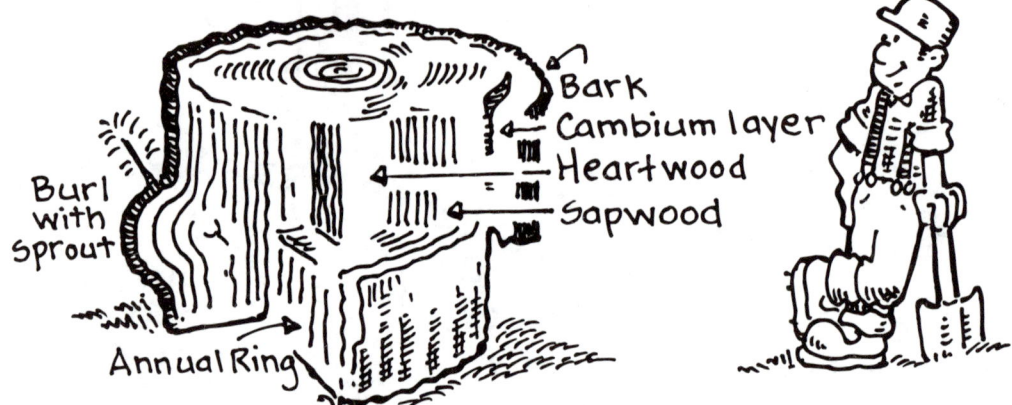

1 Study the diagram and answer the question. What is the center of a redwood tree trunk called?

- A sapwood
- B heartwood
- C cambium layer
- D burl with sprout

THINK ABOUT THE ANSWER

Option B, heartwood, is correct. Sapwood (option A) is outside the heartwood. The cambium layer (option C) is outside the sapwood. The burl with sprout (option D) is in the outside layer of the tree.

NOW YOU TRY IT

2 Write one or more sentences to explain what the diagram tells you about the annual rings.

_____
_____
_____

Check your answer on page 109.

Graphic Information

KNOW THE SKILL: CHARTS AND GRAPHS

Charts and graphs show numerical information in a way that makes it easy to understand. Charts show columns of numbers. Pie or circle graphs divide one thing into parts and show what fraction or percentage each part is of the whole. Bar graphs are used to compare totals. Line charts compare changes over time. Many graphs use colors or patterns to show different parts. They have a legend, a small box on or near the graph, to explain what each color or pattern means.

DURING THE TEST

Read the graph or chart title, the labels, any notes, the source, and the legend. Use the information from the graph or chart to rule out incorrect answers and identify the correct answer.

TEST EXAMPLE

1. What percentage of the original redwood forests in California is gone now?
- Ⓐ 4%
- Ⓑ 45%
- Ⓒ 55%
- Ⓓ 96%

Original Redwood Forests in California: 2 million acres
Redwood Forests Now in California: 85,000 acres

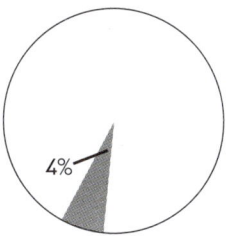

Redwood forests left standing in California

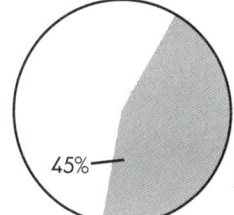

Redwoods protected in national and state parks

THINK ABOUT THE ANSWER

Option D is correct. The circle graph on the left shows that only 4% of the original forests remain (option A). That means that 96% is gone. Option B is the percentage of California's redwoods protected in the parks. Option C is the percentage of redwoods not protected in national and state parks.

NOW YOU TRY IT

2. How do these two graphs relate to each other? Which statement is true?
- Ⓕ The entire graph on the right is the same as the 4% area in the graph on the left.
- Ⓖ The entire graph on the right is the same as the 96% area in the graph on the left.
- Ⓗ The entire graph on the left is the same as the 45% area in the graph on the right.
- Ⓙ The entire graph on the left is the same as the 55% area in the graph on the right.

Check your answer on page 109.

REFERENCE SOURCES

KNOW THE SKILL: USING A GLOSSARY

A glossary is a section in the back of nonfiction, reference, and some fiction books that lists the terms in that book that might be of interest to readers. The glossary defines these terms, listing them in alphabetical order. If you encounter an unusual or unfamiliar term as you read, you can check the glossary to learn its meaning.

DURING THE TEST

For test questions related to glossaries, skim the entries shown. Then read the question and the options, and return to the glossary to eliminate incorrect options and identify the correct one.

TEST EXAMPLE

Study this section from a glossary and answer the question.

Cellulose	A white substance that forms the walls of plant cells
Condensation	Drops of water that form when mist or steam cools
Ecosystem	A group of plants and animals that interact with each other
Enzyme	A substance that helps in chemical changes without changing itself
Fossil	The remains of an animal that have turned to rock
Germinate	To sprout and start to grow
Indigenous	Plants, animals, or people who are native to a certain area
Invertebrate	An animal without a backbone

1 Find the word from this glossary that best completes this sentence: The earthworm is _____ that has no skeletal system.

Ⓐ a fossil
Ⓑ an enzyme
Ⓒ an ecosystem
Ⓓ an invertebrate

THINK ABOUT THE ANSWER

Option D is correct. An earthworm has no skeletal system, so it has no backbone. Options A, B, and C do not make sense in this sentence, based on their definitions in the glossary.

NOW YOU TRY IT

2 Does this glossary define the word *infectious*? Explain your answer.

_____

_____

Check your answer on page 109.

Reference Sources

KNOW THE SKILL: DICTIONARY ENTRY

A dictionary entry provides the spelling, pronunciation, syllabication, part of speech, definition, and sometimes synonyms and the history of a word. Knowing how to use a dictionary entry will help you on school assignments and tests and during your entire life.

DURING THE TEST

On test questions relating to dictionary entries, skim the entry first. Next, read the question, which will tell you what information to look for in the entry. Then go back to the entry and choose the correct option.

TEST EXAMPLE

Read the dictionary entry and answer the question.

de·cid·u·ous \di-'si-j -w s\ *adj* 1. falling off or shed seasonally or at a certain stage of development in the life cycle. <~leaves> <~teeth> 2. having deciduous parts. <~trees> 3. ephemeral—
de·cid·u·ous·ness *n*

1. Which word or phrase means the same as *deciduous*?
   - Ⓐ seasonally
   - Ⓑ ephemeral
   - Ⓒ having parts
   - Ⓓ development

THINK ABOUT THE ANSWER

Option B is a synonym of *deciduous*. This is the third definition of the word. The words in options A, C, and D are used to help define *deciduous*, but they are not synonyms by themselves.

NOW YOU TRY IT

2. Which of these would not be deciduous?
   - Ⓕ trees
   - Ⓖ teeth
   - Ⓗ leaves
   - Ⓙ evergreens

Check your answer on page 109.

Have a Positive Attitude
A positive attitude can help you in all that you do. Have self-confidence and expect the best to happen.

Introduction to Writing

Understanding Writing Prompts
Many tests will ask you to write several paragraphs on a topic to see how well you write. You may be asked to write fiction or nonfiction. You might describe your thoughts or feelings, or you may have to explain how to do something.

The test will usually give you a topic to write about, called a writing prompt. Here are some examples of writing prompts:

- Read a story, and then write another story like it.
- Read a story, and then predict what happens next or write about the characters.
- Write a letter or postcard as if you are on a trip to someplace you always wanted to go.
- Explain how to do something, such as riding a bicycle.
- Write about a memory, such as your first cooking lesson or your first loose tooth.
- Write about a real or fictitious person that you would like to invite to speak to your class.
- Write about something that you like or don't like, such as being the oldest, youngest, or only child in your family.
- Look at a picture and then write about it. The picture might be a rainy day, people having a quarrel, children laughing, or something else.
- Explain your opinion on a topic and give reasons for it.

Always read a writing prompt carefully so you understand what you are supposed to do. Here are some general tips before you start writing:

- If you are asked to write a story, include characters with names.
- Give your story a beginning, a middle, and an end.
- Make sure the events in the story are in the correct order.
- Think through and plan every event carefully.
- If you are asked to explain how to do something, put the steps in chronological order.
- If you are to write about a picture, tell what any people in it might feel and think.
- If you are asked to write nonfiction, include many details to support your main ideas.
- Write a draft, read it, make any necessary changes, and rewrite it.
- Read your final draft carefully. Make sure that you followed all of the instructions in the writing prompt.
- Carefully check your spelling, punctuation, language usage, and grammar.
- Use good penmanship.

Understanding Scoring Rubrics

On most proficiency or standardized tests, someone will read your writing and use a rubric to score it. Most tests use a 4-point scoring rubric. The top score in each category is 4, while 0 is the lowest. Here is what a typical rubric looks like.

Scoring Rubric

Score	Content and Ideas	Organization	Sentence Structure and Clarity	Spelling, Punctuation, Usage, and Grammar
4	Excellent, well-developed ideas	Ideas are presented in a logical order	Sentences are complete and easy to understand	No more than two mistakes
3	Most ideas are well-developed	Most ideas are in a logical order	Most sentences are complete and easy to understand	No more than five mistakes
2	Some ideas do not relate to the topic or subject	Some ideas are in order	Some sentences are complete and easy to understand	No more than seven mistakes
1	Most ideas do not relate to the topic or subject	Few ideas are in order	Few sentences are complete and easy to understand	No more than ten mistakes
0	Little or no work completed	Little or no work completed	Little or no work completed	Little or no work completed

The person scoring your writing will give you a score for each category and then add the scores. In a rubric like this one, the highest score is 16.

To score well on the writing section of a test, you must make sure your writing exactly follows what the writing prompt asks you to do. Your ideas have to be carefully thought through. You must organize them in a way that makes sense and is easy for the reader to follow. You must write in complete, error-free sentences.

Brainstorming and Organizing Your Ideas

When you are writing for a test, your time will be limited. You'll have to think clearly and quickly to organize your ideas. Graphic organizers, such as those below, can help you get started.

MAIN IDEA CHART

Your main ideas should be supported with details. This chart will help you organize your ideas and make sure you have details to back them up. You could make a chart for each main idea.

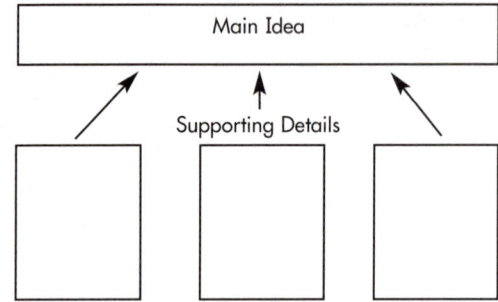

SEQUENCE CHART

A sequence chart is a good way to organize the steps in a procedure or the events in a story. Complete the chart and then write paragraphs about the topics in the order on the chart.

event on step 1
event on step 2
event on step 3
event on step 4
event on step 5

STORY PLANNER

A story planner helps you brainstorm the problem your characters will solve and how they will try to solve it.

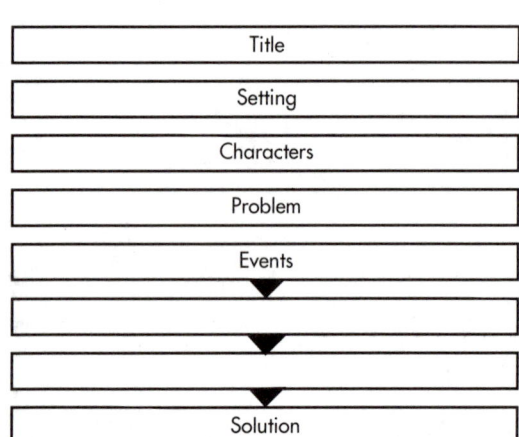

VENN DIAGRAM

If a writing prompt asks you to compare or contrast, a Venn diagram is a good way to organize likenesses (in the overlapping part) and differences (in the parts that do not overlap).

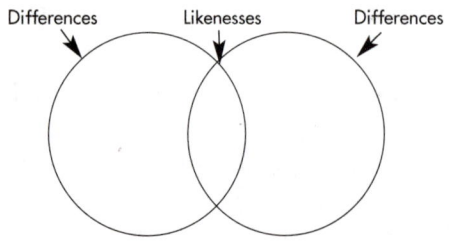

Writing Prompt and Writer's Checklist

Read the writing prompt below. Then read the checklist to make sure you understand how to score your best.

Writing Prompt

So many families have moved into the area that your community needs a new middle school. However, the only site available for the school is a park that is covered with the last large group of trees remaining in your community. Decide whether a school should be built on this land. Then write a letter to the editor of your local newspaper, persuading others to agree with your opinion. You can make up facts, if you wish, but they must be realistic.

Writer's Checklist

You will earn your best score if:

- ☐ your letter explains the situation clearly.
- ☐ you state your opinion clearly.
- ☐ you include convincing facts and reasons why your opinion is correct.
- ☐ the facts you use are realistic.
- ☐ you present your reasons in a logical order.
- ☐ you are respectful of your readers and their opinions.
- ☐ readers can easily understand your points.
- ☐ you explain what you want your readers to do.
- ☐ you include the parts of a business letter: heading (your address and the date), inside address (name/title and address of the reader, the newspaper editor in this case), salutation or greeting, body, closing, and signature.
- ☐ you make no spelling, punctuation, capitalization, or grammar errors.

Plan and Write Your First Draft

Use this graphic organizer to help you get started planning and writing your first draft.

My Opinion

Reason 1

Reason 2

Reason 3

Conclusion and Request for Action

_____

_____

_____

_____

_____

_____

PLAN AND WRITE YOUR FIRST DRAFT

Write your first draft on this page.
Use separate sheets of paper if you need more room.

_____
_____
_____
_____
_____
_____
_____
_____
_____
_____
_____
_____
_____
_____
_____

WRITE YOUR FINAL DRAFT

Before you start your final draft, use the checklist on page 33 to review your first draft. Make sure you've covered the important points in the checklist, and look for other ways to improve the content, organization, clarity, and grammar of your first draft. Then write your final draft.

_____

_____

_____

_____

_____

_____

_____

_____

_____

_____

_____

_____

_____

_____

_____

_____

_____

_____

_____

Write Your Final Draft

GIVE YOURSELF A SCORE

_____

_____

_____

_____

_____

_____

_____

Go back to the writing rubric on page 31. Use the rubic to score your work. Give yourself a score from 4 to 0 for each category. Then ask someone else to score your writing and compare the scores.

How I Scored It

Content and Ideas	Organization	Sentence Structure and Clarity	Spelling, Punctuation, Usage, and Grammar
_____	_____	_____	_____

How Someone Else Scored It

Content and Ideas	Organization	Sentence Structure and Clarity	Spelling, Punctuation, Usage, and Grammar
_____	_____	_____	_____

Introduction to Language

Language is used to express ideas. Language arts is the study of the forms and uses of language. The language arts section of a standardized test usually includes many kinds of language skills, including spelling, grammar, punctuation, and usage.

You need language skills now at school, but you will need them just as much after you graduate, at college, and at work. People with strong language skills have an easier time getting a job and keeping it. They are also much better at expressing their ideas and opinions and convincing others to agree with them.

There are ways to improve your language arts skills. Reading is the best thing you can do. Reading teaches you how people use language. Listening is important, too. You can develop an "ear for language" by listening. Read aloud and listen to books on tape. Think about "how" correct grammar and usage sounds. Then it will be easier to recognize problems with language use.

Develop your language skills by studying the following topics. You will also perform better on tests. Mastering these skills will help you understand and use language on tests and in all that you do.

- Capitalization and End Marks
- Quotation Marks
- Apostrophes
- Commas and Semicolons
- Singular and Plural Possessive Nouns
- Pronouns
- Regular and Irregular Verbs
- Verb Tenses
- Adjectives
- Adverbs
- Comparatives
- Conjunctions
- Modifiers
- Prepositions
- Sentence Formation
- Spelling

MECHANICS

KNOW THE SKILL: CAPITALIZATION AND END MARKS

Proper nouns and the first word of each sentence should begin with capital letters. Proper nouns include the names of specific people, places, events, organizations, and things. Every sentence should conclude with an end mark. A statement or command should end with a period, and a question should end with a question mark. A sentence expressing strong emotion should end with an exclamation point.

DURING THE TEST

Check to see if the name of something or someone specific is a proper noun that should be capitalized. As you read each sentence, decide whether it is a statement, a command, an exclamation, or a question. Then you will know what kind of end mark is required.

TEST EXAMPLE

1. Choose the sentence that uses the correct capitalization and end mark.
   - A) today Mr. Stevens will hand back the spelling tests that we took on friday.
   - B) Today mr. stevens will hand back the spelling tests that we took on Friday!
   - C) Today Mr. Stevens will hand back the spelling tests that we took on Friday.
   - D) today Mr. Stevens will hand back the Spelling Tests that we took on Friday?

THINK ABOUT THE ANSWER

The answer is C. In option A, *today* should be capitalized as the first word in the sentence, and *friday* should be capitalized as a proper noun. In option B, *mr. stevens*, a proper noun, should be capitalized. This sentence does not express strong emotion, so it should not end with an exclamation point. In option D, *today* should be capitalized, but *Spelling Tests* is not a proper noun, so it should not be capitalized. This sentence is not a question; it is a statement that should end with a period.

NOW YOU TRY IT

2. Choose the sentence that uses the correct capitalization and end mark.
   - F) my friend asked if I had ever visited the White House in Washington, D.C!
   - G) My friend asked if I had ever visited the White House in Washington, D.C.
   - H) My Friend asked if I had ever visited the white house in Washington, D.C.
   - J) My friend asked if I had ever visited the white house in washington, D.C?

Check your answer on page 109.

Don't Prepare at the Last Minute

Give yourself time to relax before the test. Studying up to the last minute may make you tense. Trying to learn new things right before the test might confuse you about things you already know. Feeling relaxed will help you handle the test with confidence.

MECHANICS

Language

KNOW THE SKILL: QUOTATION MARKS

Pairs of quotation marks are used to enclose the exact words that people say. A comma should separate the speaker's words from the rest of the sentence. Sometimes a sentence tells what someone said, but not in the speaker's exact words. For example: *He said that he would be late.* This is an indirect quotation that does not require quotation marks.

DURING THE TEST

Make sure that direct quotations are enclosed in quotation marks and that quotation marks are not used for indirect quotations. Then check that the commas and other punctuation in the sentence are also correct.

TEST EXAMPLE

1. Choose the sentence that is punctuated correctly.
   - Ⓐ Christa asked, "Do you think Alexander will be in our group?"
   - Ⓑ Christa asked, "Do you think Alexander will be in our group?
   - Ⓒ Christa asked "Do you think Alexander will be in our group?"
   - Ⓓ Christa asked "whether Alexander would be in our group?"

THINK ABOUT THE ANSWER

The answer is A. Option B is missing the closing quotation mark. Option C should have a comma after *asked*. Option D is an indirect quotation and should not have quotation marks. It is also a statement, not a question, so it should end with a period.

NOW YOU TRY IT

2. Choose the sentence that is punctuated correctly.
   - Ⓕ Jeb said that "if we meet him after school, he'll walk home with us."
   - Ⓖ "If you meet me after school," Jeb said, "I'll walk home with you."
   - Ⓗ "If you meet me after school" Jeb said "I'll walk home with you."
   - Ⓙ "If you meet me after school Jeb said I'll walk home with you."

Check your answer on page 109.

Get Testwise

Get a Good Night's Sleep
Go to bed early the night before the test. Your brain and body need sleep to perform their best, so don't stay up late!

Advantage Test Prep Grade 6 © 2004 Creative Teaching Press

MECHANICS

KNOW THE SKILL: COMMAS AND SEMICOLONS

Remember that an independent clause has a subject and verb and can stand alone as a sentence. When a sentence includes two independent clauses, they can be joined with a comma and a conjunction (*and, but, so, or*). Or they can be joined with a semicolon. Using a comma by itself or no punctuation at all, however, is incorrect. Look at these examples:

> Correct: My report is due tomorrow, so I'll write the last draft tonight.
> Correct: My report is due tomorrow; I'll write the last draft tonight.
> Incorrect: My report is due tomorrow, I'll write the last draft tonight.
> Incorrect: My report is due tomorrow I'll write the last draft tonight.

DURING THE TEST

When a sentence contains two independent clauses, pay special attention to how they are joined. Eliminate any choices that use a comma without a conjunction or use no punctuation at all.

TEST EXAMPLE

1. Choose the sentence that is punctuated correctly.
   - Ⓐ Denver is a long drive from here Route 70 makes it an easy trip.
   - Ⓑ Denver is a long drive from here, Route 70 makes it an easy trip.
   - Ⓒ Denver is a long drive from here but Route 70 makes it an easy trip.
   - Ⓓ Denver is a long drive from here, but Route 70 makes it an easy trip.

THINK ABOUT THE ANSWER

The answer is option D, which combines the two independent clauses with a comma and a conjunction. Option A runs the clauses together with no punctuation, while option B has a comma but needs a conjunction. Option C has a conjunction but needs a comma.

NOW YOU TRY IT

2. Choose the sentence that is punctuated correctly.
   - Ⓕ I'll meet you at Kerry's house it's the second one from the corner.
   - Ⓖ Our last unit was about arachnids; I learned a lot about spiders.
   - Ⓗ Spiders make good pets for me, I am allergic to furry animals.
   - Ⓙ Don't be late, we're going to leave right at three o'clock.

Check your answer on page 109.

Study with a Group

Form a small study group with members of your class so you can prepare for tests together. After each test, you can use what you have learned to brainstorm new preparation strategies as a group.

Mechanics

KNOW THE SKILL: APOSTROPHES

Apostrophes are used to show ownership: That is the *dog's* dish. They are also used to replace missing letters in contractions: *It's* time for dinner. You will learn more about using apostrophes to show ownership in the next lesson, Nouns. This lesson will help you use apostrophes in contractions. Here are some common contractions:

Common Contractions

it's	it is	they're	they are	he's	he is	they've	they have
can't	cannot	isn't	is not	I'll	I will	she'd	she would

DURING THE TEST

As you read, make sure all contractions have an apostrophe in the correct place.

TEST EXAMPLE

1 Choose the answer that correctly completes the sentence.
James and Kari said _____ get there before us.

- Ⓐ they
- Ⓑ theyd
- Ⓒ they'd
- Ⓓ they'ld

THINK ABOUT THE ANSWER

Option C is the answer. It's a contraction of *they would*. Option A is missing a helping verb. Option B is missing an apostrophe, and option D is misspelled.

NOW YOU TRY IT

2 Choose the answer that correctly completes the sentence.
_____ almost time for baseball practice to start.

- Ⓕ Its
- Ⓖ Its'
- Ⓗ It's
- Ⓙ It'll

Check your answer on page 109.

Keep Moving!

If one test question seems a lot harder than the others and is taking you a lot of time, skip it. You can come back to it after you have worked on easier questions. Make sure you come back and answer the ones you skipped before the end of the test time.

Grammar and Usage

KNOW THE SKILL: NOUNS

To show that something belongs to a noun, we use the possessive form. Here are the rules: For a singular noun, you add an apostrophe and s: the *girl's* eyes.

For plural nouns that end with s, you usually add just an apostrophe: the *boys'* shoes.

For plural nouns that do not end with s, you add an apostrophe and s: the *people's* voices.

DURING THE TEST

First, decide whether the noun is singular or plural. If it's plural, check to see if it ends with s. Then you will know which plural form is correct.

TEST EXAMPLE

1. Choose the correct form of the possessive noun that best completes the sentence.
   The _____ noses were red from the cold wind.
   - Ⓐ children
   - Ⓑ childrens
   - Ⓒ children's
   - Ⓓ childrens'

THINK ABOUT THE ANSWER

The answer is C. *Children* is a plural noun, but it does not end with s, so 's is added to it to make it possessive. Option A is a plural noun, but it is not possessive. Option B is an incorrect plural form. Option D has the apostrophe in the wrong place.

NOW YOU TRY IT

2. Choose the correct form of the possessive noun that best completes the sentence.
   All the _____ boundaries were not clearly marked.
   - Ⓕ ranchs
   - Ⓖ ranchs'
   - Ⓗ ranches'
   - Ⓙ ranch'es

Check your answer on page 109.

Guess the Answer

Before reading the options, guess the answer. Often you will find an answer that matches your guess.

GRAMMAR AND USAGE

KNOW THE SKILL: PRONOUNS

Pronouns replace nouns so you don't have to repeat the same nouns over and over. Pronouns should match the nouns they are replacing. If the noun is singular *(car)*, the pronoun should be singular *(it)*. If the noun is plural *(cars)*, the pronoun should be plural *(they)*. If a singular noun names a male *(the boy)*, the pronoun should be male *(he, him,* or *his)*. If a singular noun names a female *(Jane)*, the pronoun should be female *(she, her,* or *hers)*.

DURING THE TEST

Check to make sure pronouns match the nouns they replace. First, determine whether the noun is singular or plural, male or female. Then you can rule out incorrect options and choose the correct one.

TEST EXAMPLE

1. Choose the answer that best completes the sentence.
   The bears were almost invisible in the mist, but we could see _____ getting closer.
   - A it
   - B her
   - C him
   - D them

THINK ABOUT THE ANSWER

The answer is D. The pronoun *them* replaces *bears,* a plural noun. Options A, B, and C are all singular. When a noun is plural, you do not have to worry about whether it is male or female. *They, them,* and *their* can replace both male and female nouns.

NOW YOU TRY IT

2. Choose the answer that best completes the sentence.
   Mrs. Green and her husband live next door. _____ have lived in our apartment building even longer than we have.
   - F They
   - G She
   - H I
   - J He

Check your answer on page 109.

Get Comfortable

Make sure you are sitting comfortably in your chair. Keep your shoulders straight and relaxed. When you need to, talk to your teacher about taking a movement break.

Grammar and Usage

KNOW THE SKILL: REGULAR AND IRREGULAR VERBS

A regular verb is made past tense by adding *-ed* (*walk* becomes *walked*). Sometimes the spelling must be slightly changed, such as changing *y* to *i* before adding the *-ed* (*carry* becomes *carried*) or doubling the final consonant before adding the *-ed* (*drop* becomes *dropped*). In contrast, an irregular verb does not form the past tense by adding *-ed*. Instead, the spelling of the verb changes in significant ways (*bring* becomes *brought*).

DURING THE TEST

Read the sentence with each of the four verb options. One will sound right and make sense. The others will not—and you'll have your answer. When you're answering a question about verb tense, always ask yourself the key question: *When does the action of the verb take place?*

TEST EXAMPLE

1. Choose the correct verb to complete the sentence.
   Have you _____ for your ticket yet?
   - Ⓐ payd
   - Ⓑ paid
   - Ⓒ paied
   - Ⓓ payed

THINK ABOUT THE ANSWER

Option B is correct. *Pay* is an irregular verb, so its spelling changes to form the past tense. Options A, C, and D are all misspellings.

NOW YOU TRY IT

2. Choose the correct verb to complete the sentence.
   Jill _____ a dollar in the hallway, but she did not see anyone drop it.
   - Ⓕ founded
   - Ⓖ finded
   - Ⓗ found
   - Ⓙ find

Check your answer on page 109.

Don't Be Absurd!
Absurd choices are usually wrong, so you can quickly rule them out.

Grammar and Usage

KNOW THE SKILL: **VERB TENSES**

The tense of a verb tells when something happened. You can use the verb tense to indicate that something happened in the past (*worked*), is happening now (*works*), will happen (*will work*), started and ended in the past (*had been working*), started in the past and continues (*has been working*), and so on.

DURING THE TEST

As you decide on the correct verb tense for a sentence, ask yourself when the action happened. Then choose the verb option that correctly indicates when the action happened.

TEST EXAMPLE

1 Choose the correct verb to complete the sentence.
Judy _____ the apple tomorrow.
- Ⓐ had been eating
- Ⓑ will eat
- Ⓒ eats
- Ⓓ ate

THINK ABOUT THE ANSWER

Option B is correct. Judy *will eat* the apple in the future, tomorrow. Options A, C, and D do not make sense in this sentence. Option A suggests that she had been eating the apple when something else happened. Option C indicates that she is eating it now. Option D says she ate the apple in the past.

NOW YOU TRY IT

2 Choose the correct verb to complete the sentence.
I _____ to do my social studies homework last night!
- Ⓕ have been forgetting
- Ⓖ will forget
- Ⓗ forget
- Ⓙ forgot

Check your answer on page 109.

Trust Your Instincts

If you have a hunch about an answer, it is likely to be correct. Don't second-guess your decisions and change your answers unless you have a very good reason to believe you made a mistake.

GRAMMAR AND USAGE

KNOW THE SKILL: ADJECTIVES

Adjectives are descriptive words that tell how something looks, sounds, smells, feels, and/or tastes. They can also tell what kind and how many. Skillfully used, adjectives can give life to your writing. The most descriptive adjectives are specific, not general. For example, it's easier for readers to visualize a *glowing* sunset than a *beautiful* one.

DURING THE TEST

Think about whether each option tells about the noun. The best adjective will create a clear image in your mind.

TEST EXAMPLE

1. Choose the best adjective to complete the sentence.
   The clouds overhead looked _____.
   - Ⓐ dark
   - Ⓑ thick
   - Ⓒ important
   - Ⓓ threatening

THINK ABOUT THE ANSWER

Option D is correct. *Threatening* creates a clearer image than *dark* (option A) or *thick* (option B). *Threatening* is more specific and appropriate here than *important* (option C).

NOW YOU TRY IT

2. Choose the best adjective to complete the sentence.
   My first spoonful told me that the soup tasted _____.
   - Ⓕ bad
   - Ⓖ salty
   - Ⓗ awful
   - Ⓙ terrible

Check your answer on page 109.

Dress Comfortably
Some classrooms are warm and some are cool, so consider dressing in layers. That way, you can be comfortable no matter what the conditions.

Grammar and Usage

KNOW THE SKILL: ADVERBS

Adverbs describe verbs, adjectives, and other adverbs. They tell *how, when, where,* or *how often*. Remember that most—but not all—adverbs end in *-ly*. Be careful not to use an adjective where an adverb is needed. For example, a tired athlete walks *slowly*, not *slow*. Keep in mind that *good* and *well* are often confused and are often in tests. *Good* is an adjective, while *well* is an adverb.

DURING THE TEST

Questions about abverbs often include options that are adjectives. These are wrong. Eliminate the options that are adjectives, then consider which adverb makes the most sense in the sentence.

TEST EXAMPLE

1 Choose the best adverb to complete the sentence.
Kevin knows this topic _____.
- Ⓐ well
- Ⓑ fine
- Ⓒ okay
- Ⓓ good

THINK ABOUT THE ANSWER

Option A is correct. *Well* is an adverb that tells *how* Kevin knows the topic. Options B, C, and D are adjectives.

NOW YOU TRY IT

2 Choose the best adverb to complete the sentence.
Sheila described the map quickly and _____.
- Ⓕ good
- Ⓖ complete
- Ⓗ completely
- Ⓙ more completely

Check your answer on page 109.

Build Your Stamina
Some standardized tests can last for hours, so practice concentrating for a long time. Then you will be better prepared for a demanding test.

Grammar and Usage

KNOW THE SKILL: COMPARATIVES

You can compare things using adjectives or adverbs. To compare two things, add *-er* to short adjectives *(higher)* and adverbs *(faster)* or use the word *more* with longer adjectives *(more beautiful)* and adverbs *(more accurately)*. To compare more than two things, add *-est* to short adjectives *(harshest)* and adverbs *(hardest)*. Use the word *most* to form the comparative of longer adjectives *(most adventurous)* and adverbs *(most successfully)*.

DURING THE TEST

First, figure out how many things are being compared. Then determine whether the adjective or adverb is relatively long or short. Then you will be ready to eliminate wrong answers and choose the correct option.

TEST EXAMPLE

1 Select the best option to complete the sentence.
My aunt is one of the _____ people I know.
- Ⓐ courageous
- Ⓑ courageousest
- Ⓒ most courageous
- Ⓓ more courageous

THINK ABOUT THE ANSWER

Option C is correct. This sentence compares more than two things: the aunt and all other people. The word *courageous* is a relatively long adjective, so *most courageous* is the correct option. Option A does not make a comparison. Option B is not a word, while option D compares only two things.

NOW YOU TRY IT

2 Select the best option to complete the sentence.
I think leaving at 8:00 would be _____ than waiting until 8:15.
- Ⓕ wiser
- Ⓖ wisest
- Ⓗ more wise
- Ⓙ most wise

Check your answer on page 109.

Get Testwise

Choose Only from the Best Answers
Sometimes it will be obvious right away that one or more answers could not be correct. This makes your job easier. You only need to decide which of the ones that are left is the best one.

GRAMMAR AND USAGE

KNOW THE SKILL: CONJUNCTIONS

Conjunctions are words that join words or clauses and show their relationship to each other. Some conjunctions, such as *and, or, but,* and *so,* can join two independent clauses. For example: I called Henry last night, *but* he was at soccer practice. Other conjunctions, such as *because, if, when,* and *after,* can join a dependent clause to an independent one. For example: *When* I called Henry last night, he was at soccer practice.

DURING THE TEST

When you are asked to join dependent or independent clauses, read the sentence with each option. Then choose a conjunction that makes the most sense in that sentence.

TEST EXAMPLE

1 Select the best conjunction to complete the sentence.
I missed the bus this morning, _____ I had to walk to school.

- Ⓐ so
- Ⓑ or
- Ⓒ but
- Ⓓ and

THINK ABOUT THE ANSWER

Option A is correct. The second part of the sentence explains the result of the first part. The other three conjunctions do not make sense. Option B suggests there is a choice. Option C suggests that the second part of the sentence contradicts the first part. Option D suggests that the two parts of the sentence are equal ideas.

NOW YOU TRY IT

2 Select the best conjunction to complete the sentence.
_____ I find that book, I will return it to the library.

- Ⓕ But
- Ⓖ After
- Ⓗ Until
- Ⓙ Because

Check your answer on page 110.

Food for Thought

Food can affect your mood, your memory, and your ability to think. Don't eat heavy food before a test because it will make you tired. Don't skip breakfast, either! A healthful breakfast will give you the energy you need to concentrate.

GRAMMAR AND USAGE

KNOW THE SKILL: **MODIFIERS**
Modifiers are descriptive words that help you modify (tell about) something. Modifiers must be placed as close as possible to whatever they are describing in a sentence.

DURING THE TEST

If a sentence is confusing, the problem may be a misplaced modifier. Choose the option that places the modifier next to the word it modifies.

TEST EXAMPLE

1. Which sentence is written correctly?
   - A The dog barked at the people as they walked by chained behind the fence.
   - B The dog chained behind the fence barked at the people as they walked by.
   - C The dog barked at the people chained behind the fence as they walked by.
   - D As the people walked by, the dog barked at them chained behind the fence.

THINK ABOUT THE ANSWER

The answer is B. The dog is chained behind the fence. Options A and C suggest that the people are chained behind the fence. Option D doesn't make clear who is behind the fence.

NOW YOU TRY IT

2. Which sentence is written correctly?
   - F The assistant pointed at the folders lying on the table.
   - G The assistant lying on the table pointed at the folders.
   - H The folders lying on the table pointed at the assistant.
   - J Lying on the table, the assistant pointed at the folders.

Check your answer on page 110.

Keep Things in Perspective
Remember that it's just a test! There are many measures of achievement, and test scores are just one of them.

GRAMMAR AND USAGE

KNOW THE SKILL: PREPOSITIONS

Prepositions are words such as *over, about, around, during, at, for,* and *with*. They are part of prepositional phrases that serve as modifiers that tell *how, what kind, when, how much,* or *where*. Examples of prepositional phrases include *to the park, under two minutes,* and *for a while*. Like other modifiers (see page 52), prepositional phrases should be placed as close as possible to whatever they describe.

DURING THE TEST

Check to see whether prepositional phrases make sense in the sentence and are placed correctly.

TEST EXAMPLE

1. Each of these sentences has a prepositional phrase. Choose the sentence that is the clearest.
   - Ⓐ When you send a card, at the bottom be sure to sign it.
   - Ⓑ When you send a card, be sure to sign it at the bottom.
   - Ⓒ At the bottom when you send a card, be sure to sign it.
   - Ⓓ When you send a card, be sure at the bottom to sign it.

THINK ABOUT THE ANSWER

Option B is correct. *At the bottom* tells *where* to sign the card and should follow the words *to sign it*. Options A, C, and D have the prepositional phrase in places that confuse the meaning of the sentence.

NOW YOU TRY IT

2. Each of these sentences has a prepositional phrase. Choose the sentence that is the clearest.
   - Ⓕ I will look to the library for the latest mystery when I go.
   - Ⓖ I will look for the latest mystery to the library when I go.
   - Ⓗ I will look for the latest mystery when I go to the library.
   - Ⓙ To the library I will look for the latest mystery when I go.

Check your answer on page 110.

All of the Above
If "All of the above" is an option, make sure that all the options are correct before selecting it.

Grammar and Usage

KNOW THE SKILL: SENTENCE FORMATION

Complete sentences have at least one subject and one verb and offer a complete thought. Incomplete sentences, or fragments, are missing either the subject or the verb. Run-on sentences are another kind of error. They consist of two complete sentences (independent clauses) that have been joined with just a comma or with no punctuation.

DURING THE TEST

Look for the subject and verb in each group of words. If one or both are missing, it's a fragment. If two complete sentences are incorrectly joined, it's a run-on.

TEST EXAMPLE

1 Which of the following is a complete sentence?
- A   I enjoy scary movies, I don't get to see many of them.
- B   The latest one about the alien from Mars?
- C   That one was my favorite.
- D   Green hair and six eyes!

THINK ABOUT THE ANSWER

Option C is correct. The subject is *one*, and the verb is *was*. Option A is a run-on. Options B and D are fragments, lacking verbs.

NOW YOU TRY IT

2 Which of the following is not a complete sentence?
- F   I can't find the main idea in this passage.
- G   Supposed to teach a lesson.
- H   Did you find one yet?
- J   I'll read it again.

Check your answer on page 110.

Get Testwise

Fill in the Circle Completely
When you fill in your answers in your test booklet, make sure you fill in the circles all the way. Don't go outside the circles. This way you can be sure that your answers will be scored correctly.

Spelling

KNOW THE SKILL: EASILY CONFUSED WORDS

Homophones are words that sound the same but are spelled differently and have different meanings. Here are some examples: *principle/principal*, *too/two/to*, and *capital/capitol*.

DURING THE TEST

Before you can choose the correct spelling of a homophone, you must use the rest of the sentence to figure out the meaning that is meant to be used. Then look through the options for the spelling with that meaning. You can eliminate any options that are misspelled.

TEST EXAMPLE

1. Choose the option with the correct spelling to complete the sentence.
   This grocery store sells pears by their _____.
   - Ⓐ wait
   - Ⓑ wayt
   - Ⓒ wieght
   - Ⓓ weight

THINK ABOUT THE ANSWER

Option D is correct. This sentence refers to how much the pears weigh. Option A is a homophone that means "to stay until something happens." Options B and C are misspellings of the two homophones.

NOW YOU TRY IT

2. Choose the option with the correct spelling to complete the sentence.
   Blood returns to the heart through a _____.
   - Ⓕ vein
   - Ⓖ vane
   - Ⓗ vain
   - Ⓙ vayn

Check your answer on page 110.

Beware!
Beware of overly obvious or simple answers. They may be misleading.

Spelling

KNOW THE SKILL: COMPOUND WORDS

A compound word is formed from two or more short words. Compound words can be written as one word (*homework*), a hyphenated word (*thirty-one*), or two separate words (*peanut butter*).

DURING THE TEST

Check the spelling of compound words in a dictionary, if you are permitted. Otherwise, knowing whether they are spelled correctly is mostly a matter of memorization.

TEST EXAMPLE

1. Choose the option with the correct spelling to complete the sentence.
   They decided to clean out the garage _____.
   - A themselfs
   - B themselves
   - C them selves
   - D them-selves

THINK ABOUT THE ANSWER

Option B is correct. Option A is misspelled. *Themselves* is a compound word, making options C and D incorrect.

NOW YOU TRY IT

2. Choose the option with the correct spelling to complete the sentence.
   Make sure your reference sources are _____.
   - F uptodate
   - G up to date
   - H up to-date
   - J up-to-date

Check your answer on page 110.

Pick One Answer

Select only one answer for each question. If you fill in two answers, you will be marked wrong.

56   Advantage Test Prep Grade 6 © 2004 Creative Teaching Press

Introduction to Math

Mathematics is important to everyday life. It is also important to many jobs. Understanding mathematics gives you an edge in logical reasoning, problem solving, and the ability to think in abstract ways. Most standardized and proficiency tests include a mathematics section that tests many kinds of math skills.

This section of the workbook will help you develop your math skills and perform better on tests. Mastering these skills will help you understand and use math successfully on tests and in all that you do:

- Read and Write Whole Numbers and Decimals in Expanded Form
- Compare and Order Fractions, Decimals, and Common Percents
- Exponential Notation
- Add and Subtract Fractions and Mixed Numbers
- Add and Subtract Positive and Negative Numbers
- Multiply and Divide Decimals
- Multiply and Divide Fractions and Mixed Numbers
- Multiply and Divide Positive and Negative Numbers
- Order of Operations
- Estimate to Predict Results
- Greatest Common Factor
- Least Common Multiple
- Prime Factorization
- Circumference
- Classify Triangles
- Sum of the Angles of a Triangle
- Length, Weight, and Capacity
- Congruent and Similar Figures
- Use Variables
- Equations and Inequalities
- Solve One-Step and Two-Step Problems
- Estimate Solutions
- Apply Geometric Properties

NUMBER SENSE AND NUMERATION

KNOW THE SKILL: READ AND WRITE WHOLE NUMBERS AND DECIMALS IN EXPANDED FORM

A number is in expanded form when it is represented as a sum of the values of its digits. The expanded form for 397,408.25 is (3 × 100,000) + (9 × 10,000) + (7 × 1,000) + (4 × 100) + (8 × 1) + (2 × 0.1) + (5 × 0.01).

DURING THE TEST

To find the expanded form for a number, write the number in a place value chart. Find the value of each digit and write the number as the sum of the values.

TEST EXAMPLE

1 The value of the digit 4 in 6,018,527.943 is _____.
- Ⓐ 40
- Ⓑ 4
- Ⓒ 0.4
- Ⓓ 0.04

THINK ABOUT THE ANSWER

Option D is correct. The place names and place values for the decimals are tenths (0.1), hundredths (0.01), thousandths (0.001), ten thousandths (0.0001), and so on. To find the value of a digit in a number, multiply the digit by its place value. So, the value of the digit 4 is 4 × 0.01, or 0.04.

NOW YOU TRY IT

2 The expanded form for 29,060.5 is _____.
- Ⓕ (2 × 10,000) + (9 × 1,000) + (6 × 10) + (5 × 0.1)
- Ⓖ (2 × 10,000) + (9 × 1,000) + (6 × 100) + (5 × 0.01)
- Ⓗ (2 × 100,000) + (9 × 10,000) + (6 × 10) + (5 × 0.01)
- Ⓙ (2 × 1,000) + (9 × 100) + (6 × 10) + (5 × 10)

Check your answer on page 110.

Be Prepared!

If you show up prepared, you will be better able to focus. Arrive early, and make sure to bring everything you need. Bring pencils and pens, some paper, and a calculator and dictionary, if allowed. Wear a watch so you can keep track of time. If your watch beeps, turn the sound off.

NUMBER SENSE AND NUMERATION

KNOW THE SKILL: COMPARE AND ORDER FRACTIONS, DECIMALS, AND PERCENTS

To compare fractions, write equivalent fractions with the same denominators. To compare decimals, align the decimal points. Then compare digits from left to right until they are different. To compare percents, change the percents to decimals.

DURING THE TEST

Keep in mind that numbers can be written in different ways. For example, $2/5$ is the same as 40% and 0.4 or 0.40. In questions like the ones below, change all the numbers to the same form of expression (all fractions, all decimals, or all percents). This change will make it easier to compare the different numbers.

TEST EXAMPLE

1. Which number is the greatest?
   - Ⓐ $3/8$
   - Ⓑ 0.38
   - Ⓒ 37%
   - Ⓓ $7/20$

THINK ABOUT THE ANSWER

Option B is correct. Change all numbers to decimals. Option A ($3/8$) is equivalent to 0.375. Option B is already in decimal form. Option C (37%) written as a decimal is 0.37. Option D ($7/20$) is equivalent to 0.35. The decimals are 0.375, 0.38, 0.37, and 0.35. The greatest decimal is 0.38.

NOW YOU TRY IT

2. Which group of numbers is written in order from least to greatest?
   - Ⓕ $9/25$, 30%, 0.4
   - Ⓖ 30%, 0.4, $9/25$
   - Ⓗ 0.4, $9/25$, 30%
   - Ⓙ 30%, $9/25$, 0.4

Check your answer on page 110.

Ask for Help

A teacher may not be able to help you answer a test question. The idea behind a test is to see what you can do on your own. Even so, ask for help if you do not understand the directions or if you need something.

Number Sense and Numeration

KNOW THE SKILL: EXPONENTIAL NOTATION

Sometimes a number is written as the product of repeated factors. For example, 8 = 2 x 2 x 2. When a factor is repeated, the product can be written using an exponent. In exponential notation, the number being multiplied is called the base. The exponent tells how many times the number is multiplied by itself. In this example, 2 is the base and 3 is the exponent. We read this as "two to the third power," or "two cubed."

$$2 \times 2 \times 2 = 2^3 = 8$$

DURING THE TEST

You may be asked to evaluate expressions containing exponential notation or you may be asked to write a product using exponents.

TEST EXAMPLE

1. Which expression does NOT have a value of 144?
   - Ⓐ 12^2
   - Ⓑ $4^2 \times 3^2$
   - Ⓒ $2^4 \times 3^2$
   - Ⓓ $3^3 \times 2^3$

THINK ABOUT THE ANSWER

The correct answer is D. Write each expression as a product of factors and evaluate. Options A, B, and C all have a value of 144. The value of option D is 27 x 8, or 216.

NOW YOU TRY IT

2. $5^2 \times 2^5 =$ _____
   - Ⓕ 100
   - Ⓖ 800
   - Ⓗ 10,000,000
   - Ⓙ 10,000,000,000

Check your answer on page 110.

The Factors Count
When you are working with exponents, make sure you use the exponents correctly to show the number of times each factor occurs.

COMPUTATION AND OPERATIONS

KNOW THE SKILL: ADD AND SUBTRACT FRACTIONS AND MIXED NUMBERS

If fractions have like denominators, add or subtract the numerators. Write the answer in simplest form.

To add fractions with unlike denominators, such as $1/3$ and $3/4$, rewrite the fractions so that they have like denominators by finding the least common denominator (LCD). Since 12 is the LCD for 3 and 4, multiply both the numerator and denominator of $1/3$ by 4, and the numerator and denominator of $3/4$ by 3.

$$4/12 + 9/12 = 13/12$$

DURING THE TEST

Remember to write equivalent fractions if you have unlike denominators. When adding mixed numbers, add the fractions, add the whole numbers, and simplify the answer. When subtracting mixed numbers, you may have to rename fractions so that you can subtract easily.

TEST EXAMPLE

1. $4\frac{5}{6} + 3\frac{1}{3} = $ _____

   Ⓐ $7\frac{1}{6}$ Ⓒ $8\frac{1}{6}$
   Ⓑ $7\frac{2}{3}$ Ⓓ $8\frac{2}{3}$

THINK ABOUT THE ANSWER

Option C is correct answer. The LCD of the denominators is 6. Rewrite $\frac{1}{3}$ with a denominator of 6 by multiplying both the numerator and denominator by 2. $4\frac{5}{6} + 3\frac{2}{6} = 7\frac{7}{6}$; rewrite $\frac{7}{6}$ as $1\frac{1}{6}$ and add it to the 7. The final answer is $8\frac{1}{6}$.

NOW YOU TRY IT

2. $5\frac{9}{10} - 2\frac{2}{5} = $ _____

   Ⓕ $3\frac{1}{5}$ Ⓗ $3\frac{1}{2}$
   Ⓖ $3\frac{2}{5}$ Ⓙ $3\frac{7}{10}$

Check your answer on page 110.

Double Check
You can check your answer to an addition problem by subtracting one of the addends from the sum. You should get the other addend. You can check your answer to a subtraction problem by adding the difference to the number that you subtracted.

COMPUTATION AND OPERATIONS

KNOW THE SKILL: ADD AND SUBTRACT POSITIVE AND NEGATIVE NUMBERS

Positive and negative numbers are also known as integers.
The sum of two positive integers is a positive integer. $8 + 3 = 11$
The sum of two negative integers is a negative integer. $^-5 + (^-2) = ^-7$

To find the sum of integers with different signs, pretend the signs aren't there. Subtract the smaller number from the larger number. Use the sign of the larger number as the sign of the sum.

$6 + (^-13) =$ _____. $13 - 6 = 7$. Since 13 is negative, the sum is negative.
$6 + (^-13) = ^-7$.

When subtracting integers, you can rewrite subtraction as addition because subtracting a number is the same as adding its opposite.

$10 - (^-4) =$ _____
$10 - (^-4) = 10 + (^+4) = 14$

DURING THE TEST

Use a number line. Locate the first number. Move to the right if the second number is $^+$. Move to the left if the second number is $^-$. The sum is the number at the last location.

TEST EXAMPLE

1 $^-15 - (^-8) =$ _____   Ⓐ $^-23$ Ⓑ $^-7$ Ⓒ 7 Ⓓ 23

THINK ABOUT THE ANSWER

Option B is the correct answer. First rewrite the subtraction as addition. $^-15 - (^-8) = ^-15 + (^+8)$. The numbers without the signs are 15 and 8. Subtract $15 - 8 = 7$. Since 15 is negative, the sum is negative. $^-15 - (^-8) = ^-7$.

NOW YOU TRY IT

2 $^-7 + (^-16) =$ _____   Ⓕ $^-23$ Ⓖ $^-9$ Ⓗ 9 Ⓙ 23

Check your answer on page 110.

Ask Older Friends
Ask older students in your school to share some of their test-taking strategies with you. They may have experience that you could learn from to help you do your best.

COMPUTATION AND OPERATIONS

KNOW THE SKILL: MULTIPLY AND DIVIDE DECIMALS

You multiply decimals just like you multiply whole numbers. The only difference is that you must correctly place the decimal point in the product. Count the number of places to the right of the decimal point in each factor. Place the decimal point in the product so that the number of places after the decimal point is the same as the total number of places after the decimal points in both factors.

To divide a decimal by a decimal, move the decimal point in the divisor all the way to the right. Count the number of places the decimal point was moved. Move the decimal point of the dividend the same number of places to the right. Now you can divide by a whole number.

DURING THE TEST

When multiplying decimals, it's helpful to use an estimate to decide where to place the decimal point in the product.

When dividing a decimal by a whole number, remember to place the decimal point in the quotient right above the decimal point in the dividend.

TEST EXAMPLE

1 8.4 x 3.7 = _____   Ⓐ 12.1   Ⓑ 24.28   Ⓒ 30.08   Ⓓ 31.08

THINK ABOUT THE ANSWER

The correct answer is option D. Since there is one decimal place in each of the factors, there are two decimal places in the product. 8.4 is about 8 and 3.7 is about 4. Since 8 x 4 = 32, option D is a reasonable answer.

NOW YOU TRY IT

2 7.2 ÷ 0.45 = _____   Ⓕ 0.0625   Ⓖ 1.6   Ⓗ 16   Ⓙ 160

Check your answer on page 110.

Neatness Matters

If your 3's look like 8's or your 7's look like 1's or 4's, you may get a problem incorrect. Take the time to write legibly.

COMPUTATION AND OPERATIONS

KNOW THE SKILL: MULTIPLY AND DIVIDE FRACTIONS AND MIXED NUMBERS

To multiply fractions, multiply the numerators, multiply the denominators, and then write the answer in simplest form. To multiply mixed numbers, first change the mixed numbers to improper fractions.

$2\frac{1}{4} \times 1\frac{1}{2} = $ _____

Write $2\frac{1}{4}$ as $\frac{9}{4}$ and $1\frac{1}{2}$ as $\frac{3}{2}$. The sentence now looks like this:

$\frac{9}{4} \times \frac{3}{2} = \frac{27}{8}$

$\frac{27}{8}$ can be changed into a mixed number by dividing 27 by 8. Write the remainder as the numerator of a fraction. $\frac{27}{8} = 3\frac{3}{8}$.

DURING THE TEST

First change all mixed numbers to improper fractions. Rewrite problems involving division as multiplication problems using the reciprocal of the divisor.

TEST EXAMPLE

1 $3\frac{3}{5} \times \frac{2}{3} = $ _____   Ⓐ $2\frac{2}{5}$ Ⓑ $3\frac{2}{5}$ Ⓒ $4\frac{2}{5}$ Ⓓ $5\frac{2}{5}$

THINK ABOUT THE ANSWER

Option A is correct. Change $3\frac{3}{5}$ to the improper fraction $\frac{18}{5}$. Then multiply $\frac{18}{5} \times \frac{2}{3}$. Multiply the numerators, $18 \times 2 = 36$. Multiply the denominators, $5 \times 3 = 15$. $\frac{36}{15}$ can be simplified to $2\frac{6}{15}$ or $2\frac{2}{5}$.

NOW YOU TRY IT

2 $3\frac{1}{3} \div \frac{5}{8} = $ _____   Ⓕ $\frac{3}{16}$ Ⓖ $2\frac{1}{12}$ Ⓗ $3\frac{8}{15}$ Ⓙ $5\frac{1}{3}$

Check your answer on page 110.

Is a Pencil Grip for You?
If it is hard for you to hold a pencil properly, you may want to use a pencil grip. It is a piece of rubber or plastic that slips over a pencil to make it easier to hold. A pencil grip can help keep your hand from getting sore when you write a lot.

COMPUTATION AND OPERATIONS

KNOW THE SKILL: MULTIPLY AND DIVIDE POSITIVE AND NEGATIVE NUMBERS

Patterns can help you understand how to multiply integers. Since multiplication and division are related, you can divide integers by thinking of the related multiplication problem.

3 x 2 = 6   The product of two positive numbers is a positive number.

2 x (⁻3) = ⁻6   The product of a positive number and a negative number is a negative number.

⁻2 x (⁻3) = 6   The product of two negative numbers is a positive number.

DURING THE TEST

Remember these rules for multiplying and dividing integers:
    If the signs are the same, the product or quotient is positive.
    If the signs are different, the product or quotient is negative.

TEST EXAMPLE

1   ⁻9 x (⁻8) = _____   Ⓐ ⁻72   Ⓑ ⁻17   Ⓒ 17   Ⓓ 72

THINK ABOUT THE ANSWER

The product of 9 and 8 is 72. Since the product of two negative numbers is a positive number, option D is the correct answer.

NOW YOU TRY IT

2   56 ÷ (⁻4) = _____   Ⓕ ⁻52   Ⓖ ⁻14   Ⓗ 52   Ⓙ 14

Check your answer on page 110.

Get Testwise

Review Your Work

If you finish the test before time is up, don't leave! Use every minute allowed to check your work. Quickly make sure that you have answered all the questions. Check your answer sheet for mistakes. Double-check the placement of decimal points and commas in numbers and that you used the correct sign for integers.

Advantage Test Prep Grade 6 © 2004 Creative Teaching Press

COMPUTATION AND OPERATIONS

KNOW THE SKILL: ORDER OF OPERATIONS

Order of operations is a set of rules. Using these rules, you will get the same answer that everyone else gets when evaluating an expression.
1. Compute inside parentheses.
2. Evaluate exponents.
3. Multiply or divide in order from left to right.
4. Add or subtract in order from left to right.

DURING THE TEST

A mnemonic device for remembering the order of operations is the nonsense word PEMDAS. The P stands for parentheses, E for exponents, M for multiply, D for divide, A for add, and S for subtract.

TEST EXAMPLE

1. $7 + 3^2 \times (6 - 4) = $ _____
   - Ⓐ 25
   - Ⓑ 32
   - Ⓒ 57
   - Ⓓ 200

THINK ABOUT THE ANSWER

Option A is the correct choice. Using the order of operations, simplify the expression in parentheses first. Then evaluate the expression with the exponent, then multiply, then add.
$7 + 3^2 \times (6 - 4) = 7 + 3^2 \times 2 = 7 + 9 \times 2 = 7 + 18 = 25$

NOW YOU TRY IT

2. Which expression has a value of 33?
   - Ⓕ $2^3 + 3 \times 6 \div 2$
   - Ⓖ $2^3 + 3 \times (6 \div 2)$
   - Ⓗ $(2^3 + 3) \times 6 \div 2$
   - Ⓙ $(2^3 + 3 \times 6) \div 2$

Check your answer on page 110.

Get Testwise

Build on Success
Think of times you met a challenge or did something that was very hard. Keep this in mind when you are trying to meet a new challenge in school.

Estimation and Number Theory

KNOW THE SKILL: ESTIMATE TO PREDICT RESULTS

Sometimes you do not need an exact answer. In these cases, you can estimate. You can also use estimates to check the reasonableness of your computation. Here are some of the ways you can use estimates:

1. Round to estimate sums, differences, and products.
2. Use front-end estimation to estimate sums and differences.
3. Use compatible numbers to estimate sums, differences, products, and quotients.

DURING THE TEST

Here are some steps to follow when you need to estimate or predict an answer:
- First, read the whole problem carefully. Decide what operation you will use.
- Then choose an estimation method.
- Use your math skills to estimate the answer.
- Eliminate answer choices that are not near the estimate.
- Find the correct answer.

TEST EXAMPLE

1 The product of 58.3 × 4.82 is about how much?

Ⓐ 200
Ⓑ 240
Ⓒ 300
Ⓓ 3,000

THINK ABOUT THE ANSWER

Since this question does not ask for an exact answer, you can estimate. Round 58.3 to 60. Round 4.8 to 5. Multiply 60 × 5. The correct answer is option C.

NOW YOU TRY IT

2 Using compatible numbers, which is the best estimate for 7,892 ÷ 41?

Ⓕ 20
Ⓖ 100
Ⓗ 200
Ⓙ 2,000

Check your answer on page 110.

Simpler Problems

If a problem seems complicated to you, replace the numbers with simpler ones, round the numbers, or use compatible numbers. Then reread the problem and decide on a plan to solve. Then try solving the original problem.

Advantage Test Prep Grade 6 © 2004 Creative Teaching Press

ESTIMATION AND NUMBER THEORY

KNOW THE SKILL: GREATEST COMMON FACTOR

To find the common factors of two or more numbers, list all the factors of each number. The factors that are in all of the lists are the *common factors*. The largest number that is a common factor is called the *greatest common factor* or *GCF*.

Factors of 18: **1, 2, 3, 6,** 9, 18
Factors of 30: **1, 2, 3,** 5, **6,** 10, 15, 30

The greatest common factor (GCF) of 18 and 30 is 6.

DURING THE TEST

To find all the factors of a number, think of the factors in pairs.
Here's how it's done for the factors of 40:

1   2   4   5   8   10   20   40

TEST EXAMPLE

1 The greatest common factor of 15 and 45 is _____.

Ⓐ 3
Ⓑ 5
Ⓒ 15
Ⓓ 45

THINK ABOUT THE ANSWER

Options A, B and C show common factors of 15 and 45. The greatest common factor is 15. Option C is correct.

NOW YOU TRY IT

2 4 is the greatest common factor of _____.

Ⓕ 20 and 48
Ⓖ 24 and 48
Ⓗ 8 and 24
Ⓙ 8 and 48

Check your answer on page 111.

Let Your Teacher Know

If there is something bothering you, let your teacher know. Don't let noise or a broken pencil keep you from doing your best work.

ESTIMATION AND NUMBER THEORY

KNOW THE SKILL: LEAST COMMON MULTIPLE

A multiple of a number is the product of that number and a whole number. The list below shows the multiples of 7.

7, 14, 21, 28, 35, 42, 49, 56, 63, 70, . . .

You can find the common multiples of two or more numbers by finding multiples that appear in all the lists. The smallest of these common multiples is called the *least common multiple* or *LCM*.

Multiples of 5: 5, 10, 15, 20, 25, 30, 35, **40**, 45, 50, . . .
Multiples of 8: 8, 16, 24, 32, **40**, 48, 56, 64, 72, 80, . . .

The least common multiple (LCM) of 5 and 8 is 40.

DURING THE TEST

When finding the LCM of two numbers, you can stop finding multiples when you find the first match. When one of the numbers is a factor of the other, the greater number will be the least common multiple.

TEST EXAMPLE

1 The least common multiple of 12 and 8 is _____.

- Ⓐ 2
- Ⓑ 4
- Ⓒ 24
- Ⓓ 96

THINK ABOUT THE ANSWER

Options A and B are factors of 12 and 8, not multiples. Options C and D are common multiples of 12 and 8. The least common multiple is 24. Option C is correct.

NOW YOU TRY IT

2 36 is the least common multiple of _____.

- Ⓕ 6 and 18
- Ⓖ 4 and 9
- Ⓗ 3 and 12
- Ⓙ 2 and 18

Check your answer on page 111.

Helpful Hints

Don't confuse the GCF and the LCM. The greatest common factor of two numbers will always be less than or equal to the smaller number. The least common multiple of two numbers will always be greater than or equal to the greater number.

Advantage Test Prep Grade 6 © 2004 Creative Teaching Press

Estimation and Number Theory

KNOW THE SKILL: PRIME FACTORIZATION

A *prime number* is a counting number that has only two factors, itself and 1. A *composite number* is a counting number greater than 1 that has more than two factors. A composite number can be written as the product of prime numbers. This is called the *prime factorization* of the number.

You can find the prime factorization of a number by making a factor tree. First, find any pair of factors. Then find pairs of factors for the factors until all the factors are prime numbers. For example, here are two different factor trees for 24. Notice that even though this example begins with a different pair of factors, it ends with the same prime factorization.

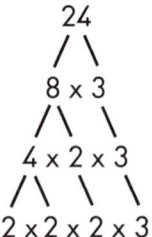

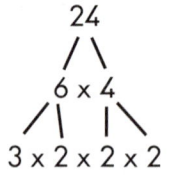

```
      24                              24
     / \                             / \
    8 x 3                           6 x 4
   /|  |                           /| | |
  4 x 2 x 3                       3 x 2 x 2 x 2
 /| | | |
2 x 2 x 2 x 3      24 = 2³ x 3              24 = 2³ x 3
```

DURING THE TEST

If you are asked to find the prime factorization of an even number, you know that one of the prime factors must be 2 or a power of 2. Make sure all the factors in the prime factorization are prime numbers.

TEST EXAMPLE

1 The prime factorization of 72 is _____.

Ⓐ 2×6^2
Ⓑ $2^2 \times 3^3$
Ⓒ $2^2 \times 3 \times 6$
Ⓓ $2^3 \times 3^2$

THINK ABOUT THE ANSWER

Option D is correct. Options A, C, and D show factorizations for 72, but only option D shows the prime factorization. Option B shows the prime factorization for 108.

NOW YOU TRY IT

2 $2^2 \times 5^2$ is the prime factorization of _____.

Ⓕ 25
Ⓖ 49
Ⓗ 100
Ⓙ 625

Check your answer on page 111.

Keep Your Answer Sheet Neat

Make sure to keep your answer sheet smooth and free of extra marks. It will make your paper easier to grade and help you get the score you deserve.

MEASUREMENT

KNOW THE SKILL: CIRCUMFERENCE

The distance around a circle is called its *circumference*. The *diameter* of circle is the line segment through the center of the circle with endpoints on the circle. The *radius* of a circle is a line segment from the center of the circle to a point on the circle. The length of the diameter of a circle is twice the length of the radius of the circle.

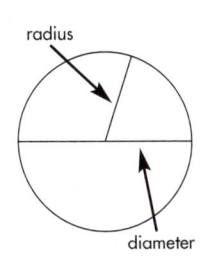

The ratio of the circumference, C, to the diameter, d, of any circle is always the same. The Greek letter π is used to name the ratio C/d. An approximation of the value of π is 3.14. Sometimes the fraction $^{22}/_7$ is used as the value of π.

If you know the length of the diameter of a circle, you can use the formula C = πd to find the circumference. If you know the length of the radius, you can use the formula C = 2πr to find the circumference.

DURING THE TEST

The circumference of a circle is an approximate answer. You may have to round your answer if required. If the length of the radius or diameter is a multiple of 7, use $^{22}/_7$ for π. Otherwise, use 3.14 for π.

TEST EXAMPLE

1. Which is the best approximation for the circumference of this circle?

   Ⓐ 18.84 in.
   Ⓑ 37.68 in.
   Ⓒ 75.36 in.
   Ⓓ 56.4 in.

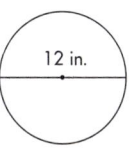

THINK ABOUT THE ANSWER

The correct answer is option B. The formula for the circumference of a circle if you know the diameter is C = πd. Since 12 is not a multiple of 7, use 3.14 for π. 3.14 × 12 = 37.68.

NOW YOU TRY IT

2. A circle has a circumference of 88 inches. What is the radius of the circle?

   Ⓕ 7 in.   Ⓗ 21 in.
   Ⓖ 14 in. Ⓙ 28 in.

Check your answer on page 111.

Work Backwards

Sometimes it is easier to solve a problem by substituting the multiple-choice responses into a formula and seeing which one works.

MEASUREMENT

KNOW THE SKILL: CLASSIFY TRIANGLES

You can classify triangles based on the measures of their angles.
- In an *acute triangle*, all angles measure less than 90°.
- In a *right triangle*, one angle measures exactly 90°.
- In an *obtuse triangle*, one angle measures more than 90°.

You can also classify triangles based on the lengths of their sides.
- In an *equilateral triangle*, all three sides are the same length.
- In an *isosceles triangle*, two sides are the same length.
- In a *scalene triangle*, the three sides all have different lengths.

DURING THE TEST

If you are given a drawing of a triangle, don't assume that it is drawn to scale. Don't guess any answer based on the drawing. Use the measurements given for the angles or the sides to classify the triangle.

TEST EXAMPLE

1 A triangle is an obtuse triangle. Its angle measures could be _____.
- Ⓐ 40°, 50°, 90°
- Ⓑ 100°, 30°, 50°
- Ⓒ 80°, 80°, 20°
- Ⓓ 45°, 45°, 90°

THINK ABOUT THE ANSWER

Use the definition of an obtuse triangle. The only choice that has an angle that measures more than 90° is option B.

NOW YOU TRY IT

2 The sides of a triangle have lengths of 8 in., 5 in., and 8 in. It is a(n) _____.
- Ⓕ scalene triangle
- Ⓖ equilateral triangle
- Ⓗ isosceles triangle
- Ⓙ right triangle

Check your answer on page 111.

Keep Learning New Terms

Continually expand your math vocabulary. Make flash cards with illustrations for any terms you have trouble remembering.

MEASUREMENT

KNOW THE SKILL: SUM OF THE ANGLES OF A TRIANGLE

Triangles come in many different shapes and sizes, but there is one thing that all triangles have in common. The sum of the measures of the three angles is always 180°. You can show this by drawing and cutting out a triangle. Then tear off the three corners of the triangle and line up the angles. Do you see that the three angles line up to form a straight angle? Since the measure of a straight angle is 180°, the sum of the angles of a triangle must also be 180°.

DURING THE TEST

You may be given the measures of two angles of a triangle and asked to find the third angle. To do this, find the sum of the two given angles and subtract the sum from 180°. You may be given three angle measures and asked if it is possible to draw a triangle with the given measures. If the measures of the three angles add up to 180°, a triangle can be drawn.

TEST EXAMPLE

1. The measures of two angles of a triangle are 56° and 62°. The measure of the third angle is _____.

   A) 56°
   B) 62°
   C) 68°
   D) 118°

THINK ABOUT THE ANSWER

The correct answer is option B. The sum of the measures of the two given angles is 56 + 62 = 118. Subtract 118 from 180. 180 − 118 = 62. So the measure of the third angle is 62°.

NOW YOU TRY IT

2. Which of the following sets of measures will NOT form a triangle?

   F) 110°, 35°, 45°
   G) 43°, 85°, 52°
   H) 60°, 50°, 70°
   J) 75°, 30°, 75°

   Check your answer on page 111.

Get Testwise

Watch Out for Opposites

Sometimes, a test answer will look right but will have a word like *not* or *no* that makes it mean the opposite. Don't let opposite answers confuse or mislead you.

Advantage Test Prep Grade 6 © 2004 Creative Teaching Press

73

MEASUREMENT

KNOW THE SKILL: LENGTH, WEIGHT, AND CAPACITY

Customary Units of Length	Metric Units of Length
1 foot (ft) = 12 inches (in.) 1 yard (yd) = 3 feet 1 mile (mi) = 5,280 feet 1 kilometer (km) = 1,000 meters	1 centimeter (cm) = 10 millimeters (mm) 1 meter (m) = 1,000 millimeters 1 meter = 100 centimeters
Customary Units of Weight	Metric Units of Mass
1 pound (lb) = 16 ounces (oz) 1 ton (T) = 2,000 pounds	1 gram (g) = 1,000 milligrams (mg) 1 kilogram (kg) = 1,000 grams
Customary Units of Capacity	Metric Units of Capacity
1 cup (c) = 8 fluid ounces 1 pint (pt) = 2 cups 1 quart (qt) = 2 pints 1 gallon (gal) = 4 quarts	1 liter (L) = 1,000 milliliters (mL)

DURING THE TEST

You may be asked to identify the unit of measure for an object, or a reasonable estimate for the measurement of an object. You may be asked to change from one unit of measure to another. Look for a table like the one above to find the relationship between the two units of measure.

TEST EXAMPLE

1. Which would you use to measure the length of a pen?
   - A   grams
   - B   meters
   - C   centimeters
   - D   kilometers

THINK ABOUT THE ANSWER

The question asks for a unit of length. Right away you can eliminate option A, since the gram is a unit of mass. A benchmark for a meter is the length of a baseball bat. A benchmark for a centimeter is the width of your fingernail. A benchmark for a kilometer is how far you can walk in about 15 minutes. Option C is the correct choice.

NOW YOU TRY IT

2. The number of inches in 6 feet is _____.
   - F   0.5
   - G   50
   - H   60
   - J   72

Check your answer on page 111.

Geometry

KNOW THE SKILL: CONGRUENT AND SIMILAR FIGURES

When two figures are congruent, they have the same size and the same shape. The corresponding sides and the corresponding angles are congruent.

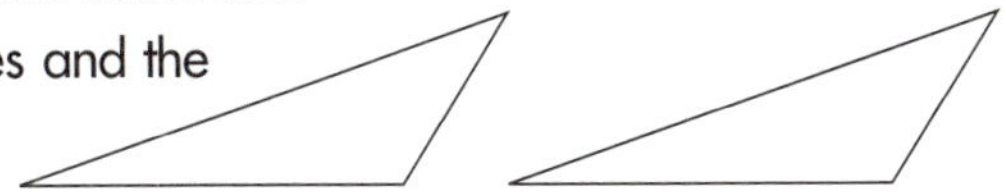

When two figures are similar, they have the same shape but not necessarily the same size. The corresponding sides are in proportion and the corresponding angles are congruent.

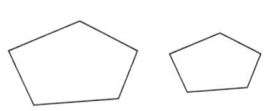

DURING THE TEST

You may be asked to recognize congruent or similar figures. You may also be asked to identify the corresponding parts of congruent or similar figures.

TEST EXAMPLE

1 Which pair of figures is congruent?

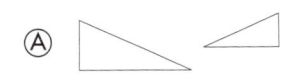

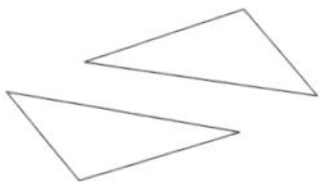

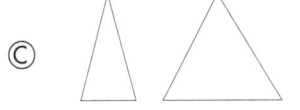

Ⓐ   Ⓒ
Ⓑ   Ⓓ

THINK ABOUT THE ANSWER

The correct answer is option B. The triangles in option A are similar but not congruent triangles. The triangles in option C are not congruent or similar. The rectangles in option D are not congruent or similar.

NOW YOU TRY IT

2 The figures are similar. Which angle corresponds to angle C?

Ⓕ angle W
Ⓖ angle X
Ⓗ angle Y
Ⓙ angle Z

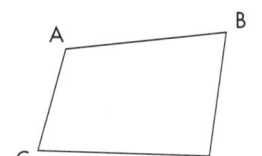

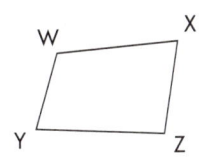

Check your answer on page 111.

Get Testwise

Trace It
Sometimes it is helpful to trace a figure, cut it out, and rotate it to see if two figures are congruent.

ALGEBRAIC THINKING, DATA ANALYSIS, PROBABILITY

KNOW THE SKILL: USE VARIABLES

A letter that represents a number is called a *variable*. An algebraic expression contains one or more variables and/or numbers. When you evaluate an algebraic expression, you substitute a number for the variable in the expression.

Expression	Evaluate if $n = 8$.
$n + 5$	$8 + 5 = 13$
$n - 2$	$8 - 2 = 6$
$6n$	$6 \times 8 = 48$
$n/2$	$8/2 = 4$

DURING THE TEST

You may be asked in a test question to use a variable to represent a quantity. Sometimes, you may be told the value of the variable and asked to evaluate an expression, as in the table above.

TEST EXAMPLE

1. Maya is three years younger than Kieran. If a represents Kieran's age, which of the following represents Maya's age?
   - Ⓐ $3a$
   - Ⓑ $a + 3$
   - Ⓒ $3 - a$
   - Ⓓ $a - 3$

THINK ABOUT THE ANSWER

The correct answer is option D. The variable a represents Kieran's age and since Maya is 3 years younger, you have to subtract 3 from Kieran's age, a.

NOW YOU TRY IT

2. What is the value of the expression $3n + 4$ if $n = 2$?
   - Ⓕ 10
   - Ⓖ 14
   - Ⓗ 30
   - Ⓙ 36

Check your answer on page 111.

Get Testwise

Word Meanings

Think about other meanings of words if you don't understand a math term. For example, if you can't remember what the word *variable* means, think of how the word is used in another context. In weather, you may have heard about variable winds, which means changing winds. In math, a variable is a symbol that can have changing values.

ALGEBRAIC THINKING, DATA ANALYSIS, PROBABILITY

KNOW THE SKILL: EQUATIONS AND INEQUALITIES

An equation is a mathematical sentence that shows two expressions are equal. An equation may have a variable in it. To solve an equation for the variable, you want to get the variable alone on one side of the equation. You can do this by using inverse operations. Addition and subtraction are inverse operations. Multiplication and division are inverse operations. An inequality is also a mathematical sentence. However, the equals sign is replaced by either one of the following symbols: < or >.

DURING THE TEST

You may be asked to find the solution to an equation or inequality. You may be asked to identify an equation that can be used to solve a problem. Some tests may ask you to solve equations and inequalities and explain your reasoning in writing. Here is how to solve some equations and inequalities.

$n + 5 = 13$	$y - 9 < 6$
$n + 5 - 5 = 13 - 5$	$y - 9 + 9 < 6 + 9$
$n = 8$	$y < 15$
$5a > 35$	$\frac{w}{6} = 8$
$\frac{5a}{5} > \frac{35}{5}$	$6(\frac{w}{6}) = 6(8)$
$a > 7$	$w = 48$

TEST EXAMPLE

1. The students in the Environmental Club at Pines Middle School are going on a field trip to the aquarium. The admission cost for the aquarium is $9 per student. Which equation can be used to find how many students can go to the aquarium if a total of $306 is collected?

   Ⓐ $s + 9 = 306$
   Ⓑ $9s = 306$
   Ⓒ $306 - s = 9$
   Ⓓ $s/9 = 306$

THINK ABOUT THE ANSWER

The correct answer is option B. If each ticket costs $9, then multiplying 9 times the number of students will give the total amount collected, $306.

NOW YOU TRY IT

2. Which equation does not have a solution of 15?

   Ⓕ $3y = 45$
   Ⓖ $y - 7 = 8$
   Ⓗ $y/5 = 3$
   Ⓙ $y + 6 = 9$

   Check your answer on page 111.

Check Mate!

Always check the solution by replacing the value you got for the variable in the original problem.

Advantage Test Prep Grade 6 © 2004 Creative Teaching Press

Problem Solving

KNOW THE SKILL: SOLVE ONE-STEP AND TWO-STEP PROBLEMS

The following steps can help you decide how to solve a word problem:
1. Read the problem carefully.
2. Analyze the information given.
3. Decide on a plan for solving the problem.
4. Do the math and check your answer.

DURING THE TEST

Study the table below to help you decide which operation to use for certain situations.

Use addition when you need to find: • a total amount when each part is given • a result when a number is increased	Use subtraction when you need to find: • how much greater or less one number is than another • a result when a number is decreased • how much is left after an amount is used
Use multiplication when you need to find: • a total when you are given several amounts that are equal	Use division when you need to find: • an amount split into equal parts • an average

Some word problems may require more than one operation, as shown in the examples below.

TEST EXAMPLE

1. A piece of wood is 8 feet long. If Keiko cuts off two pieces of wood that are each $3\frac{1}{4}$ feet long, how long will the remaining piece be?

   Ⓐ $1\frac{1}{2}$ feet
   Ⓑ $1\frac{3}{4}$ feet
   Ⓒ $4\frac{3}{4}$ feet
   Ⓓ $6\frac{1}{2}$ feet

THINK ABOUT THE ANSWER

The correct answer is option A. You first need to figure out how many feet of wood Keiko cut off in all. You can do this by multiplying $2 \times 3\frac{1}{4}$, which is $6\frac{1}{2}$. Then subtract $6\frac{1}{2}$ from 8. $8 - 6\frac{1}{2} = 1\frac{1}{2}$, so the remaining piece will be $1\frac{1}{2}$ feet long.

NOW YOU TRY IT

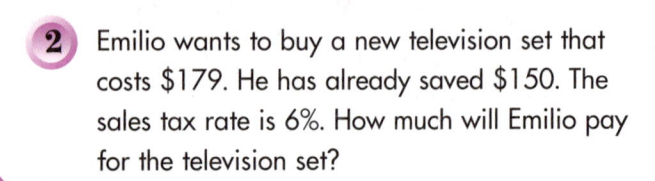

2. Emilio wants to buy a new television set that costs $179. He has already saved $150. The sales tax rate is 6%. How much will Emilio pay for the television set?

   Ⓕ $29.00
   Ⓖ $159.00
   Ⓗ $185.00
   Ⓙ $189.74   Check your answer on page 111.

Get Testwise

Step by Step

If you need to use more than one operation to solve a problem, work in steps, using one operation at a time.

Problem Solving

KNOW THE SKILL: ESTIMATE SOLUTIONS

Estimation is a way of getting an answer quickly or checking that your answer is reasonable. You may want to overestimate, that is get an answer that is greater than the exact answer, to make sure you have enough time, money, or space. You may want to underestimate, that is get an answer that is less than the exact answer, if you need to place an order and you don't know how much you already have on hand.

DURING THE TEST

Look for key words in the problem that tell you that you don't need an exact answer. Some words that mean to estimate are *about* and *approximate*.

TEST EXAMPLE

1. Marina wants to buy a head of lettuce for $1.29, a bunch of grapes for $2.79, a cantaloupe for $1.89, and some chicken for $3.75. She only has $8 in her wallet. About how much more money does she need?

- Ⓐ $1
- Ⓑ $2
- Ⓒ $3
- Ⓓ $4

THINK ABOUT THE ANSWER

The key word in the problem is *about*. You do not need an exact answer, so round each amount to the nearest dollar. $1.29 is about $1, $2.79 is about $3, $1.89 is about $2, and $3.75 is about $4. $1 + $3 + $2 + $4 = $10, so Marina needs about $2 more. The correct choice is option B.

NOW YOU TRY IT

2. Paul's bedroom is 11 feet wide and 14 feet long. Which is the best estimate for the total cost of the tile if the tile costs $2.99 per square foot?

- Ⓕ $150
- Ⓖ $300
- Ⓗ $420
- Ⓙ $450

Check your answer on page 111.

Get Testwise

Use Units Correctly

Make sure you understand the difference between the perimeter and area of a figure and that you know the correct units for expressing them. Area is expressed in square units. Volume is expressed in cubic units.

Problem Solving

KNOW THE SKILL: APPLY GEOMETRIC PROPERTIES

Some geometric properties that you can apply to the real world are *similarity* and *symmetry*. When two figures are similar, they have the same shape but their sizes may be different. The corresponding sides of similar figures are in proportion. A figure has *line symmetry* if it can be folded along a line so that the two halves exactly match. A figure has *turn symmetry* if you can turn it less than one full rotation and you match the original exactly.

DURING THE TEST

If you are given similar figures and need to find an unknown length, write and solve a proportion. To determine if a figure has line symmetry, fold it in various ways to see if you can get the two folded parts to match. To determine if a figure has turn symmetry, rotate it and keep turning until it matches the original exactly.

TEST EXAMPLE

1 A tree that is 6 feet tall casts a shadow that is 4 feet long. How high is a flagpole that casts a shadow 12 feet long at the same time?

Ⓐ 14 feet
Ⓑ 16 feet
Ⓒ 18 feet
Ⓓ 20 feet

THINK ABOUT THE ANSWER

Option C is right. The triangles are similar. You can write a proportion comparing the height of each object to its shadow. Let f represent the height of the flagpole. Then $6/4 = f/12$. Solving the proportion, $f = 18$.

NOW YOU TRY IT

2 Which of the following does not have line symmetry?

Ⓕ A   Ⓗ T
Ⓖ S   Ⓙ W

Check your answer on page 111.

Your Scratch Paper

You may be given paper or a space in your text booklet to do your figuring. This can be a helpful place to test things out and show your math thinking to yourself before you choose an answer.

Practice Test Introduction

The rest of this book is a practice test. It's a lot like a standardized test you might have to take for school. It includes all of the skills you have studied in this book. The questions on the test are similar to the ones you've been practicing.

The test is divided into the same sections as the earlier parts of the book: reading, writing, language arts, and math. Use the answer sheets on the next two pages for recording your answers for each section. The answer sheet is divided in the same way as the practice test itself, with four sections. Here are some tips to keep in mind as you take the practice test:

- Don't worry if you're a little nervous. In fact, being a little nervous can sometimes help you to do your best.
- Remember the Get Testwise suggestions you read at the bottom of each practice page. They can help you on the practice test, just like they can help you on the real thing.
- Make sure you understand all the directions before you start the test. Ask an adult if you have any questions about the directions.
- Unlike a real standardized test, there's no time limit on this practice test. However, try to work quickly, but not so quickly that you make mistakes. Practice managing your time.
- If you don't know an answer, you can guess at it or skip it and come back to it later.
- Try to complete a whole test section, such as reading or math, at one time. You will see a stop sign in the bottom right corner of the page when you come to the end of a test section.
- After finishing each section, check your answers. You'll find the answers at the back of the book, starting on page 112.

Student Information Sheet

Complete this student information sheet. It is similar to ones found on tests. Be sure to fill in the correct bubble for each letter of your name.

STUDENT'S NAME																
LAST										FIRST						MI
Ⓐ	Ⓐ	Ⓐ	Ⓐ	Ⓐ	Ⓐ	Ⓐ	Ⓐ	Ⓐ	Ⓐ	Ⓐ	Ⓐ	Ⓐ	Ⓐ	Ⓐ	Ⓐ	Ⓐ
Ⓑ	Ⓑ	Ⓑ	Ⓑ	Ⓑ	Ⓑ	Ⓑ	Ⓑ	Ⓑ	Ⓑ	Ⓑ	Ⓑ	Ⓑ	Ⓑ	Ⓑ	Ⓑ	Ⓑ
Ⓒ	Ⓒ	Ⓒ	Ⓒ	Ⓒ	Ⓒ	Ⓒ	Ⓒ	Ⓒ	Ⓒ	Ⓒ	Ⓒ	Ⓒ	Ⓒ	Ⓒ	Ⓒ	Ⓒ
Ⓓ	Ⓓ	Ⓓ	Ⓓ	Ⓓ	Ⓓ	Ⓓ	Ⓓ	Ⓓ	Ⓓ	Ⓓ	Ⓓ	Ⓓ	Ⓓ	Ⓓ	Ⓓ	Ⓓ
Ⓔ	Ⓔ	Ⓔ	Ⓔ	Ⓔ	Ⓔ	Ⓔ	Ⓔ	Ⓔ	Ⓔ	Ⓔ	Ⓔ	Ⓔ	Ⓔ	Ⓔ	Ⓔ	Ⓔ
Ⓕ	Ⓕ	Ⓕ	Ⓕ	Ⓕ	Ⓕ	Ⓕ	Ⓕ	Ⓕ	Ⓕ	Ⓕ	Ⓕ	Ⓕ	Ⓕ	Ⓕ	Ⓕ	Ⓕ
Ⓖ	Ⓖ	Ⓖ	Ⓖ	Ⓖ	Ⓖ	Ⓖ	Ⓖ	Ⓖ	Ⓖ	Ⓖ	Ⓖ	Ⓖ	Ⓖ	Ⓖ	Ⓖ	Ⓖ
Ⓗ	Ⓗ	Ⓗ	Ⓗ	Ⓗ	Ⓗ	Ⓗ	Ⓗ	Ⓗ	Ⓗ	Ⓗ	Ⓗ	Ⓗ	Ⓗ	Ⓗ	Ⓗ	Ⓗ
Ⓘ	Ⓘ	Ⓘ	Ⓘ	Ⓘ	Ⓘ	Ⓘ	Ⓘ	Ⓘ	Ⓘ	Ⓘ	Ⓘ	Ⓘ	Ⓘ	Ⓘ	Ⓘ	Ⓘ
Ⓙ	Ⓙ	Ⓙ	Ⓙ	Ⓙ	Ⓙ	Ⓙ	Ⓙ	Ⓙ	Ⓙ	Ⓙ	Ⓙ	Ⓙ	Ⓙ	Ⓙ	Ⓙ	Ⓙ
Ⓚ	Ⓚ	Ⓚ	Ⓚ	Ⓚ	Ⓚ	Ⓚ	Ⓚ	Ⓚ	Ⓚ	Ⓚ	Ⓚ	Ⓚ	Ⓚ	Ⓚ	Ⓚ	Ⓚ
Ⓛ	Ⓛ	Ⓛ	Ⓛ	Ⓛ	Ⓛ	Ⓛ	Ⓛ	Ⓛ	Ⓛ	Ⓛ	Ⓛ	Ⓛ	Ⓛ	Ⓛ	Ⓛ	Ⓛ
Ⓜ	Ⓜ	Ⓜ	Ⓜ	Ⓜ	Ⓜ	Ⓜ	Ⓜ	Ⓜ	Ⓜ	Ⓜ	Ⓜ	Ⓜ	Ⓜ	Ⓜ	Ⓜ	Ⓜ
Ⓝ	Ⓝ	Ⓝ	Ⓝ	Ⓝ	Ⓝ	Ⓝ	Ⓝ	Ⓝ	Ⓝ	Ⓝ	Ⓝ	Ⓝ	Ⓝ	Ⓝ	Ⓝ	Ⓝ
Ⓞ	Ⓞ	Ⓞ	Ⓞ	Ⓞ	Ⓞ	Ⓞ	Ⓞ	Ⓞ	Ⓞ	Ⓞ	Ⓞ	Ⓞ	Ⓞ	Ⓞ	Ⓞ	Ⓞ
Ⓟ	Ⓟ	Ⓟ	Ⓟ	Ⓟ	Ⓟ	Ⓟ	Ⓟ	Ⓟ	Ⓟ	Ⓟ	Ⓟ	Ⓟ	Ⓟ	Ⓟ	Ⓟ	Ⓟ
Ⓠ	Ⓠ	Ⓠ	Ⓠ	Ⓠ	Ⓠ	Ⓠ	Ⓠ	Ⓠ	Ⓠ	Ⓠ	Ⓠ	Ⓠ	Ⓠ	Ⓠ	Ⓠ	Ⓠ
Ⓡ	Ⓡ	Ⓡ	Ⓡ	Ⓡ	Ⓡ	Ⓡ	Ⓡ	Ⓡ	Ⓡ	Ⓡ	Ⓡ	Ⓡ	Ⓡ	Ⓡ	Ⓡ	Ⓡ
Ⓢ	Ⓢ	Ⓢ	Ⓢ	Ⓢ	Ⓢ	Ⓢ	Ⓢ	Ⓢ	Ⓢ	Ⓢ	Ⓢ	Ⓢ	Ⓢ	Ⓢ	Ⓢ	Ⓢ
Ⓣ	Ⓣ	Ⓣ	Ⓣ	Ⓣ	Ⓣ	Ⓣ	Ⓣ	Ⓣ	Ⓣ	Ⓣ	Ⓣ	Ⓣ	Ⓣ	Ⓣ	Ⓣ	Ⓣ
Ⓤ	Ⓤ	Ⓤ	Ⓤ	Ⓤ	Ⓤ	Ⓤ	Ⓤ	Ⓤ	Ⓤ	Ⓤ	Ⓤ	Ⓤ	Ⓤ	Ⓤ	Ⓤ	Ⓤ
Ⓥ	Ⓥ	Ⓥ	Ⓥ	Ⓥ	Ⓥ	Ⓥ	Ⓥ	Ⓥ	Ⓥ	Ⓥ	Ⓥ	Ⓥ	Ⓥ	Ⓥ	Ⓥ	Ⓥ
Ⓦ	Ⓦ	Ⓦ	Ⓦ	Ⓦ	Ⓦ	Ⓦ	Ⓦ	Ⓦ	Ⓦ	Ⓦ	Ⓦ	Ⓦ	Ⓦ	Ⓦ	Ⓦ	Ⓦ
Ⓧ	Ⓧ	Ⓧ	Ⓧ	Ⓧ	Ⓧ	Ⓧ	Ⓧ	Ⓧ	Ⓧ	Ⓧ	Ⓧ	Ⓧ	Ⓧ	Ⓧ	Ⓧ	Ⓧ
Ⓨ	Ⓨ	Ⓨ	Ⓨ	Ⓨ	Ⓨ	Ⓨ	Ⓨ	Ⓨ	Ⓨ	Ⓨ	Ⓨ	Ⓨ	Ⓨ	Ⓨ	Ⓨ	Ⓨ
Ⓩ	Ⓩ	Ⓩ	Ⓩ	Ⓩ	Ⓩ	Ⓩ	Ⓩ	Ⓩ	Ⓩ	Ⓩ	Ⓩ	Ⓩ	Ⓩ	Ⓩ	Ⓩ	Ⓩ

SCHOOL

TEACHER

FEMALE ○ **MALE** ○

BIRTHDATE					
MONTH		DAY		YEAR	
JAN	○	⓪	⓪	⓪	⓪
FEB	○	①	①	①	①
MAR	○	②	②	②	②
APR	○	③	③	③	③
MAY	○		④	④	④
JUN	○		⑤	⑤	⑤
JUL	○		⑥	⑥	⑥
AUG	○		⑦	⑦	⑦
SEP	○		⑧	⑧	⑧
OCT	○		⑨	⑨	⑨
NOV	○				
DEC	○				

GRADE

④ ⑤ ⑥ ⑦ ⑧

Advantage Test Prep Grade 6 © 2004 Creative Teaching Press

Practice Test Answer Sheet

READING

1. Ⓐ Ⓑ Ⓒ Ⓓ
2. Ⓕ Ⓖ Ⓗ Ⓙ
3. Written answer
4. Ⓕ Ⓖ Ⓗ Ⓙ
5. Ⓐ Ⓑ Ⓒ Ⓓ
6. Ⓕ Ⓖ Ⓗ Ⓙ
7. Ⓐ Ⓑ Ⓒ Ⓓ
8. Ⓕ Ⓖ Ⓗ Ⓙ
9. Ⓐ Ⓑ Ⓒ Ⓓ
10. Ⓕ Ⓖ Ⓗ Ⓙ
11. Ⓐ Ⓑ Ⓒ Ⓓ
12. Written answer
13. Ⓐ Ⓑ Ⓒ Ⓓ
14. Ⓕ Ⓖ Ⓗ Ⓙ
15. Ⓐ Ⓑ Ⓒ Ⓓ
16. Written answer
17. Ⓐ Ⓑ Ⓒ Ⓓ
18. Written answer
19. Ⓐ Ⓑ Ⓒ Ⓓ
20. Ⓕ Ⓖ Ⓗ Ⓙ

LANGUAGE

21. Ⓐ Ⓑ Ⓒ Ⓓ
22. Ⓕ Ⓖ Ⓗ Ⓙ
23. Ⓐ Ⓑ Ⓒ Ⓓ
24. Ⓕ Ⓖ Ⓗ Ⓙ
25. Ⓐ Ⓑ Ⓒ Ⓓ
26. Ⓕ Ⓖ Ⓗ Ⓙ
27. Ⓐ Ⓑ Ⓒ Ⓓ
28. Ⓕ Ⓖ Ⓗ Ⓙ
29. Ⓐ Ⓑ Ⓒ Ⓓ
30. Ⓕ Ⓖ Ⓗ Ⓙ
31. Ⓐ Ⓑ Ⓒ Ⓓ
32. Ⓕ Ⓖ Ⓗ Ⓙ
33. Ⓐ Ⓑ Ⓒ Ⓓ
34. Ⓕ Ⓖ Ⓗ Ⓙ
35. Ⓐ Ⓑ Ⓒ Ⓓ
36. Ⓕ Ⓖ Ⓗ Ⓙ
37. Ⓐ Ⓑ Ⓒ Ⓓ
38. Ⓕ Ⓖ Ⓗ Ⓙ
39. Ⓐ Ⓑ Ⓒ Ⓓ
40. Ⓕ Ⓖ Ⓗ Ⓙ
41. Ⓐ Ⓑ Ⓒ Ⓓ
42. Ⓕ Ⓖ Ⓗ Ⓙ
43. Ⓐ Ⓑ Ⓒ Ⓓ
44. Ⓕ Ⓖ Ⓗ Ⓙ
45. Ⓐ Ⓑ Ⓒ Ⓓ
46. Ⓕ Ⓖ Ⓗ Ⓙ
47. Ⓐ Ⓑ Ⓒ Ⓓ
48. Ⓕ Ⓖ Ⓗ Ⓙ
49. Ⓐ Ⓑ Ⓒ Ⓓ
50. Ⓕ Ⓖ Ⓗ Ⓙ

MATH

51. Ⓐ Ⓑ Ⓒ Ⓓ
52. Ⓕ Ⓖ Ⓗ Ⓙ
53. Ⓐ Ⓑ Ⓒ Ⓓ
54. Ⓕ Ⓖ Ⓗ Ⓙ
55. Ⓐ Ⓑ Ⓒ Ⓓ
56. Ⓕ Ⓖ Ⓗ Ⓙ
57. Ⓐ Ⓑ Ⓒ Ⓓ
58. Ⓕ Ⓖ Ⓗ Ⓙ
59. Ⓐ Ⓑ Ⓒ Ⓓ
60. Ⓕ Ⓖ Ⓗ Ⓙ
61. Ⓐ Ⓑ Ⓒ Ⓓ
62. Ⓕ Ⓖ Ⓗ Ⓙ
63. Ⓐ Ⓑ Ⓒ Ⓓ
64. Ⓕ Ⓖ Ⓗ Ⓙ
65. Ⓐ Ⓑ Ⓒ Ⓓ
66. Ⓕ Ⓖ Ⓗ Ⓙ
67. Ⓐ Ⓑ Ⓒ Ⓓ
68. Ⓕ Ⓖ Ⓗ Ⓙ
69. Ⓐ Ⓑ Ⓒ Ⓓ
70. Ⓕ Ⓖ Ⓗ Ⓙ
71. Ⓐ Ⓑ Ⓒ Ⓓ
72. Ⓕ Ⓖ Ⓗ Ⓙ
73. Ⓐ Ⓑ Ⓒ Ⓓ
74. Ⓕ Ⓖ Ⓗ Ⓙ
75. Ⓐ Ⓑ Ⓒ Ⓓ
76. Ⓕ Ⓖ Ⓗ Ⓙ
77. Ⓐ Ⓑ Ⓒ Ⓓ
78. Ⓕ Ⓖ Ⓗ Ⓙ
79. Ⓐ Ⓑ Ⓒ Ⓓ
80. Ⓕ Ⓖ Ⓗ Ⓙ

Advantage Test Prep Grade 6 © 2004 Creative Teaching Press

Practice Test: Reading

Read the passage and then answer questions 1 through 10.

Building a New Pyramid

Not all the old pyramids are in ancient Egypt. For years, you have seen the food pyramid on milk cartons, bread wrappers, and cereal boxes. It might have seemed that this pyramid was carved in stone, much like those pyramids in Egypt. However, nutritionists—food experts—have recently decided that the food pyramid might actually be contributing to our weight problems. They are designing a new pyramid based on what researchers have learned about food.

Over recent years, studies have shown that people are eating too many refined, processed carbohydrates. They are part of the lowest, biggest level of the pyramid and include white bread and white rice. Instead, people should be eating cereals and breads made from whole grains. The new food pyramid will probably not put refined and whole-grain foods in the same carbohydrate category. Doing this encourages us to eat too much of one type and allows us to ignore the other.

Nutritionists have also been studying fats. They have learned that eating monounsaturated or polyunsaturated fats actually lowers our risk of heart disease. These healthy fats are found in vegetable oils, nuts, other plant products, and fish. They are good for our hearts.

However, eating saturated fats, found in whole milk, butter, and fatty red meat, raises cholesterol levels. This encourages heart disease. We should also eat less trans fatty acids, found in many margarines and vegetable shortening. Trans fatty acids are in many cookies, crackers, and other foods. The new food pyramid will distinguish between these different kinds of fats.

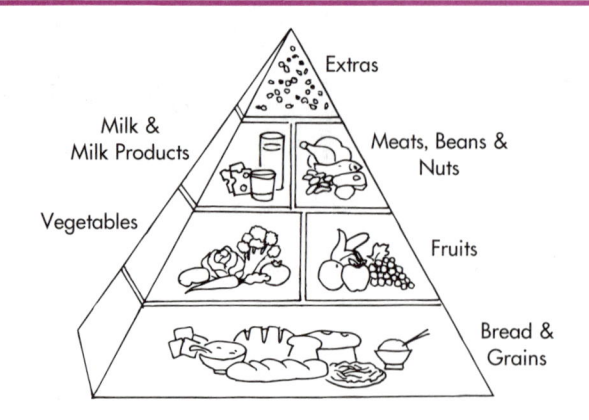

The updated pyramid will not be ready until at least 2004, but you don't have to wait that long to change your eating habits. The information on food packages right now can help you. Start with the list of ingredients. Are there any whole grains in the snack you are considering? That would be a good sign. Of course, raw fruits and vegetables, excellent sources of nutrition, do not have labels printed on them. However, you can eat lots of them and be sure you are helping your body!

Back to the food packages. Check the amount of total fat in a serving, and then see how much of that is saturated fat. Most of it? Do your heart a favor and find a different snack! Food labels do not mention trans fatty acids now, but that information may be required soon.

Now look at the amount of total carbohydrates in a serving. Do these carbohydrates include any fiber to help food move through your body—or are they mostly sugars? Do you really need to eat that much sugar?

If someone recorded and measured the food you eat every day, what would your personal food pyramid look like? You can do better! Make eating healthy foods a habit.

1. What is the main idea of this passage?
    - Ⓐ The current food pyramid is too complicated.
    - Ⓑ The current food pyramid groups too many foods together.
    - Ⓒ The current food pyramid does not mention trans fatty acids.
    - Ⓓ No one is using the current food pyramid as a guide for eating.

2. *Saturated fat* is to *heart disease* as *exercise* is to _____.
    - Ⓕ unsaturated fats
    - Ⓖ trans fatty acids
    - Ⓗ carbohydrates
    - Ⓙ good health

3. Write two or more sentences to explain whether you think the new food pyramid will have more or fewer categories of foods. Explain your answer.

    _____

    _____

    _____

4. Look at the food pyramid diagram. Why is the "Bread & Grains Group" the largest part of the pyramid?
    - Ⓕ We should eat more foods from this group than any other group.
    - Ⓖ We do eat more foods from this group than any other group.
    - Ⓗ Most of the foods available to us are in this group.
    - Ⓙ The foods in this group are the most nutritious.

5. Which of these events happened first?
    - Ⓐ Nutritionists realized that whole grains are better than refined, processed foods.
    - Ⓑ Nutritionists realized that different fats have different effects on our health.
    - Ⓒ The current food pyramid was created.
    - Ⓓ A new food pyramid was considered.

GO →

6 Which generalization is based on this passage?
- Ⓕ The current food pyramid is a valuable tool in guiding our eating habits.
- Ⓖ Nutritionists are still figuring out what we should eat to stay healthy.
- Ⓗ Nutritionists really do not know what we should eat to stay healthy.
- Ⓙ When the new pyramid is available, people will eat healthier foods.

7 The passage mentions *refined* foods. In this case, *refined* means _____.
- Ⓐ polite
- Ⓑ unprocessed
- Ⓒ manufactured
- Ⓓ exact or precise

8 What caused nutritionists to re-evaluate the food pyramid?
- Ⓕ the serving sizes on the pyramid
- Ⓖ the size of food packages
- Ⓗ discoveries about foods
- Ⓙ food labels

9 What does the shape of the food pyramid indicate?
- Ⓐ Fats, oils, and sweets are the best foods.
- Ⓑ We should eat more of some foods than others.
- Ⓒ Bread, cereal, rice, and pasta are the last foods we should eat.
- Ⓓ We should eat foods from the dairy group and the meat group at the same time.

10 If this passage had a glossary, which of these words would NOT be in it?
- Ⓕ carbohydrate
- Ⓖ cholesterol
- Ⓗ infection
- Ⓙ refined

PRACTICE TEST: READING

Read the passage and then answer questions 11 through 20.

Helping the Poor

Megan had ridden past this gray, cement-block building with her parents many times and wondered what went on inside. The building had no windows, just a green door and a small sign that said "Community Shelter."

"Come on in." Joseph smiled as he pushed open the green door. "No one will bite you." Joseph lived two houses from her. He and his dad often volunteered to serve meals at the shelter, but this was Megan's first time. Her parents had decided it was a good idea, as long as she stayed near Mr. Masselli.

The shelter was essentially one huge room, painted light yellow. Megan could see doors at the back, probably leading to the restrooms. Narrow cots were pushed against the walls, and folding chairs had been set up in a ragged semicircle. Several women sat on some of them, juggling babies and overseeing a rambunctious group of children play with an old basketball. Men huddled in small groups, talking quietly. Joseph had told her that many shelters were for men only, but this one accepted families.

It was lunchtime, so three long tables formed a row opposite the folding chairs. Different community groups took turns bringing in lunch, but they were always happy to have more servers. Megan could see that today's menu was sloppy joes with corn, fruit cocktail, and cookies. Her stomach growled, but she knew that the food was reserved for the families.

A tall, thin man with a scraggly beard glanced at Megan and said, "You can help Haley dish out the fruit cocktail, okay?" Megan nodded, but the man was already talking to someone else. She spotted enormous cans of fruit cocktail sitting near the trays of cookies.

Megan smiled nervously at a red-haired girl about her age who was standing near the cans and holding a slotted spoon. "Hi! You must be Haley. I'm Megan."

"Hi." Haley handed her a pair of thin plastic gloves. "We have to wear these," Haley explained, "so we don't get germs in the food."

Megan slipped them on. "Have you done this before?" she asked Haley.

Haley nodded as she stirred the fruit with her spoon. The families had formed a long line now and were moving along the tables, holding their plates out to each server. Megan watched how Haley let the juice drain out of the fruit before she put a big spoonful on each plate. Soon Megan could do it without spilling too much on the table. Once in a while, she glanced up at the faces in the line. Several of the adults smiled and said, "Thank you, miss," while some of the children softly begged, "More, please."

"Don't you feel sorry for these people?" Megan whispered to Haley. "I mean, they're so poor!"

Haley must not have heard because she didn't answer. Soon the cans were empty, and all the other food was gone, too. After Megan helped wipe off the tables, she wanted to say good-bye to Haley, but she didn't see her. As Megan followed Joseph and his dad out the door, she finally spotted Haley. She was sitting on a cot beside a red-haired woman who looked very much like her. Haley looked over just then and caught Megan staring, but she just smiled and hugged the woman.

Practice Test: Reading

11 With whom is Haley sitting at the end of the story?
- Ⓐ her friend
- Ⓑ her mother
- Ⓒ a former neighbor
- Ⓓ a stranger she just met

12 Write one or more sentences to explain what you think Megan will do the next time she volunteers at the shelter. Explain the reasons for your prediction.

_____

_____

_____

13 Which of these happened first?
- Ⓐ Megan was assigned to dish out the fruit cocktail.
- Ⓑ Megan realized why Haley was there.
- Ⓒ Megan and Joseph became friends.
- Ⓓ Megan met Haley.

14 What message do you think this author wanted to share with readers?
- Ⓕ You should not make assumptions about people you don't know.
- Ⓖ If you help others, you will feel good about yourself.
- Ⓗ The first time you do something is the hardest.
- Ⓙ We should all help the poor.

15 What point of view is used in this story?
- Ⓐ first person
- Ⓑ second person
- Ⓒ third person
- Ⓓ fourth person

16 What is more important about the setting of this story, the location or the time period? Write one or more sentences to explain your answer.

_____

_____

_____

17 Which of these words best describes Haley?
- Ⓐ impatient
- Ⓑ confident
- Ⓒ depressed
- Ⓓ thoughtless

18 Write two or more sentences to explain how Megan and Haley are the same and different.

_____

_____

_____

19 What is the most likely reason why Megan volunteered to help at the shelter?
- Ⓐ It was a class project.
- Ⓑ She wanted to meet Haley.
- Ⓒ Joseph encouraged her to do it.
- Ⓓ Her parents encouraged her to do it.

20 Which of these sentences best summarizes the story?
- Ⓕ At the shelter, Megan learned not to jump to conclusions about people.
- Ⓖ Megan learned how to serve lunch to homeless families at the shelter.
- Ⓗ Megan made a new friend while helping at the shelter.
- Ⓙ Megan's experience at the shelter surprised her.

Practice Test: Writing

Writing Prompt
Everyone at your school buys lunch in the cafeteria. You have a favorite lunch that you would like the cafeteria to serve. Write a letter to the school newspaper to persuade the principal, cafeteria staff, and other students that your favorite lunch would make a healthful, delicious addition to the lunch menu.

Your letter will be scored according to this checklist. After writing your first draft, review the checklist and make any needed improvements. Then write your final draft. A letter to the editor of a school newspaper probably does not need all the parts of a formal business letter.

You will earn your best score if:

- ☐ you clearly explain the reason for your letter.

- ☐ you choose a healthful lunch and describe it clearly.

- ☐ you provide strong reasons why the cafeteria should begin serving this lunch. Choose reasons that will appeal to your readers.

- ☐ you present the reasons in a logical order.

- ☐ you end by asking readers to take a specific action. In this case, you might suggest different actions for different readers.

- ☐ your letter is easy to understand.

- ☐ your letter has no errors in spelling, grammar, usage, or punctuation.

Plan Your Writing

The more planning you do now, the less revising you will have to do later. You might find this graphic organizer helpful.

My Favorite Lunch

Reason 1 Why the Cafeteria Should Serve It

Reason 2

Reason 3

Conclusion and Request for Action

_____

_____

_____

_____

GO →

Practice Test: Writing

Write Your First Draft
Use all the skills you have learned to write a first draft.

_____

_____

_____

_____

_____

_____

_____

_____

_____

_____

_____

_____

_____

_____

_____

_____

Practice Test: Writing

Write Your Final Draft
Now it's time to write your final draft. Use the writer's checklist on page 90 to make sure that you will achieve the best possible score. Carefully proofread your work when you are done.

_____

_____

_____

_____

_____

_____

_____

_____

_____

_____

_____

_____

_____

_____

_____

_____

_____

_____

_____

_____

_____

_____

_____

_____

_____

Give Yourself a Score

Go back to the writing rubric on page 31. Use the rubric to score your work. Give yourself a score from 4 to 0 for each category. Then ask someone else to score your writing and compare the scores.

How I Scored It

Content and Ideas	Organization	Sentence Structure and Clarity	Spelling, Punctuation, Usage, and Grammar
_____	_____	_____	_____

How Someone Else Scored It

Content and Ideas	Organization	Sentence Structure and Clarity	Spelling, Punctuation, Usage, and Grammar
_____	_____	_____	_____

PRACTICE TEST: LANGUAGE

For questions 21 through 28, choose the sentence that is written correctly.

21.
   - Ⓐ Did Jonas and his Friend meet at the Park on Oak Street?
   - Ⓑ Did Jonas and his friend meet at the park on Oak street.
   - Ⓒ Jonas and his Friend met at the Park on Oak street!
   - Ⓓ Jonas and his friend met at the park on Oak Street.

22.
   - Ⓕ Aaron said, "that he would be there as soon as he can."
   - Ⓖ Aaron said, "I'll be there as soon as I can."
   - Ⓗ Aaron said "I'll be there as soon as I can."
   - Ⓙ Aaron said, I'll be there as soon as I can."

23.
   - Ⓐ I was born in Ohio most of my family still lives there.
   - Ⓑ I was born in Ohio, most of my family still lives there.
   - Ⓒ I was born in Ohio; most of my family still lives there.
   - Ⓓ I was born in Ohio and most of my family still lives there.

24.
   - Ⓕ She wont get there until after the game has started.
   - Ⓖ I would'nt want to miss any of the action.
   - Ⓗ Aren't you going to come with us?
   - Ⓙ I'am trying to get another ticket.

25.
   - Ⓐ Try not to step on peoples' feet!
   - Ⓑ I finally found my dogs' lost collar.
   - Ⓒ Is that Alices book lying there on the table?
   - Ⓓ I heard children's voices out on the playground.

GO

26
- F James and Justin will sing the song he wrote together.
- G Joy and Jessica have finished her part of the project.
- H Ryan has written his first draft of the report.
- J Anthony is finishing their part tonight.

27
- A Susan brought her sister to the park.
- B Kelly sayed she would be coming later.
- C Meg comed right after her piano lesson.
- D I leaved because it was almost time for dinner.

28
- F When he handed me the cup, I accidentally drop it.
- G By the time you get there, I will be there, too.
- H Yesterday my cousin send me an e-mail.
- J We had a math test tomorrow morning.

29 Choose the best adjective to complete the sentence.
The main character in this story is a _____ person.
- A nice
- B good
- C thoughtful
- D wonderful

30 Choose the best adverb to complete the sentence.
Allison studied hard and did _____ on her social studies test.
- F fine
- G well
- H good
- J okay

Practice Test: Language

31 Choose the comparative adjective that best completes the sentence.
Sam's bookbag looks _____ than mine.
- Ⓐ heavier
- Ⓑ heaviest
- Ⓒ more heavy
- Ⓓ most heavy

32 Choose the conjunction that best completes the sentence.
I would have been here on time, _____ I couldn't find my favorite shirt.
- Ⓕ or
- Ⓖ so
- Ⓗ but
- Ⓙ and

For questions 33 through 35, choose the sentence that is written clearly and correctly.

33
- Ⓐ Barking, I took a picture of my brother and his dog.
- Ⓑ I took a barking picture of my brother and his dog.
- Ⓒ I took a picture of my barking brother and his dog.
- Ⓓ I took a picture of my brother and his barking dog.

34
- Ⓕ My uncle had a wedding at age six.
- Ⓖ At age six, my uncle had a wedding.
- Ⓗ I went to my uncle's wedding at age six.
- Ⓙ At age six, I went to my uncle's wedding.

35
- Ⓐ Time for vacation at last.
- Ⓑ Will the beach be warm and sunny this year?
- Ⓒ The car is packed we're taking more stuff than last year.
- Ⓓ A tent, sleeping bags, a kerosene stove, a lantern, and bug spray.

For questions 36 and 37, choose the correctly spelled word that best completes the sentence.

36 Juanita wants chocolate chip, but I'll take _____ vanilla.
- F playne
- G plane
- H plain
- J plan

37 To study for the test, I _____ chapters.
- A out lined twenty one
- B out-lined twenty-one
- C out-lined twentyone
- D outlined twenty-one

For questions 38 through 40, choose the sentence that is written correctly.

38
- F My Aunt works for a Company in Chicago!
- G Her company is located on South State Street.
- H Does her Company do programming for its Customers?
- J Starting in june, her Supervisor will be Henry Davidson.

39
- A Well, I have another idea," Janet said.
- B "There's a better solution to this problem" she insisted.
- C Gerald said, "We'd be glad to hear your solution. What is it?"
- D "I have to check something before I can tell you, she whispered."

40
- F Our neighbors had a baby yesterday; they named her Carin.
- G Carin already has a big brother, his name is Samuel.
- H Sam is three, he is very happy to have a baby sister.
- J Carin will be home today Sam will get to hug her.

Practice Test: Language

For questions 41 through 46, choose the correct word to complete the sentence.

41 The candidate moved through the crowd of mothers, shaking each _____ hand.
- Ⓐ womans'
- Ⓑ womens'
- Ⓒ woman's
- Ⓓ women's

42 People should always do what _____ think is right.
- Ⓕ he
- Ⓖ she
- Ⓗ you
- Ⓙ they

43 I picked that book because I _____ it would be interesting.
- Ⓐ think
- Ⓑ thank
- Ⓒ thought
- Ⓓ will think

44 I _____ waited for my sister to pick me up.
- Ⓕ quiet
- Ⓖ patient
- Ⓗ patiently
- Ⓙ impatient

45 When I was in fifth grade, I used to come here _____.
- Ⓐ oftener
- Ⓑ oftenest
- Ⓒ more often
- Ⓓ most often

46 We could wait for Tara, _____ we could go without her.
- Ⓕ or
- Ⓖ so
- Ⓗ but
- Ⓙ and

For questions 47 through 50, choose the sentence that is written correctly.

47
- Ⓐ The director at the camp asked us all to stand in a line.
- Ⓑ The director asked us all to stand in a line at the camp.
- Ⓒ The director asked us all at the camp to stand in a line.
- Ⓓ In a line, the director asked us all to stand at the camp.

48
- Ⓕ Five for your team and four for ours.
- Ⓖ Which team will be at bat first?
- Ⓗ Same rules as always.
- Ⓙ No pinch-hit batters.

49
- Ⓐ Whose name did you get in the drawing?
- Ⓑ Abigail does not know whose coming.
- Ⓒ Was that you're sister on the phone?
- Ⓓ Your ten minutes late!

50
- Ⓕ What part-of-speech is that word?
- Ⓖ I wore my heaviest sweat shirt today.
- Ⓗ Your cousin is waiting down-stairs.
- Ⓙ I counted thirty-seven steps.

Practice Test: Math

51. The angles of a triangle are given. Which is an acute triangle?
- Ⓐ 70°, 20°, 90°
- Ⓑ 25°, 105°, 50°
- Ⓒ 80°, 70°, 30°
- Ⓓ 35°, 35°, 110°

52. 300,000 + 4,000 + 700 + 2 + 0.5 + 0.09 is the expanded form for _____.
- Ⓕ 3,472.59
- Ⓖ 340,702.59
- Ⓗ 347,259
- Ⓙ 304,702.59

53. The diameter of a dinner plate is 14 inches. What is the circumference of the plate?
- Ⓐ 22 inches
- Ⓑ 44 inches
- Ⓒ 88 inches
- Ⓓ 154 inches

54. The cost of a dinner for two people was $24.75. They left a 20% tip on the cost of the dinner. There also was sales tax of $1.98. What was the total cost of the meal including tax and tip?
- Ⓕ $26.93
- Ⓖ $29.70
- Ⓗ $31.68
- Ⓙ $32.08

55. Which metric unit is most appropriate to use to measure the length of a football field?
- Ⓐ mm
- Ⓑ cm
- Ⓒ m
- Ⓓ km

GO

56 The measures of two angles of a triangle are 55° and 85°. What is the measure of the third angle of the triangle?
- Ⓕ 40°
- Ⓖ 55°
- Ⓗ 85°
- Ⓙ 140°

57 What is the value of $5x - 2$ if $x = 4$?
- Ⓐ 7
- Ⓑ 18
- Ⓒ 27
- Ⓓ 52

58 A triangle that has no sides of the same length is _____.
- Ⓕ equilateral
- Ⓖ isosceles
- Ⓗ scalene
- Ⓙ not possible

59 Which expression has a value of 46?
- Ⓐ 7 × 8 + 5 – 1
- Ⓑ 7 × (8 + 5) – 1
- Ⓒ 7 + 5 × 8 – 1
- Ⓓ (7 + 8) × 5 – 1

60 Kim danced for a number of minutes. Then she danced for 20 more minutes. Which expression shows how long Kim danced?
- Ⓕ $n + 20$
- Ⓖ $n - 20$
- Ⓗ $20 - n$
- Ⓙ $20n$

Practice Test: Math

61 The prime factorization of 75 is _____.
- Ⓐ 3 × 25
- Ⓑ 3 × 5^2
- Ⓒ 2 × 5 × 7
- Ⓓ 3^2 × 5

62 What is the greatest common factor of 12 and 27?
- Ⓕ 3
- Ⓖ 9
- Ⓗ 12
- Ⓙ 27

63 9 × ⁻6 = _____
- Ⓐ -54
- Ⓑ -3
- Ⓒ 3
- Ⓓ 54

64 Which group of numbers is written in order from least to greatest?
- Ⓕ 3/20, 20%, 0.12
- Ⓖ 0.12, 3/20, 20%
- Ⓗ 20%, 3/20, 0.12
- Ⓙ 3/20, 0.12, 20%

65 5⅔ + 3¼
- Ⓐ 8 3/7
- Ⓑ 8¼
- Ⓒ 8 11/12
- Ⓓ 9 11/12

66 Which of the following does NOT have a value of ⁻6?
- Ⓕ ⁻14 + 8
- Ⓖ ⁻12 + (⁻6)
- Ⓗ 3 − 9
- Ⓙ ⁻10 − (⁻4)

67 12.92 ÷ 3.4
- Ⓐ 0.34
- Ⓑ 0.38
- Ⓒ 3.4
- Ⓓ 3.8

68 The product of 7.82 × 29.45 is about
- Ⓕ 210
- Ⓖ 240
- Ⓗ 2,100
- Ⓙ 2,400

69 $2\frac{2}{3} \div \frac{3}{4} =$ _____
- Ⓐ $\frac{6}{32}$
- Ⓑ 2
- Ⓒ $3\frac{2}{3}$
- Ⓓ $3\frac{5}{9}$

70 The least common multiple of 9 and 15 is
- Ⓕ 3
- Ⓖ 15
- Ⓗ 45
- Ⓙ 90

PRACTICE TEST: MATH

71 Which pair of figures is congruent?

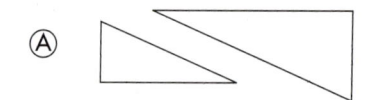

- Ⓐ
- Ⓑ
- Ⓒ
- Ⓓ

72 The number of ounces in 4 pounds is _____.
- Ⓕ 4
- Ⓖ 40
- Ⓗ 48
- Ⓙ 64

73 Claudia charges $6 per hour for babysitting. This weekend she earned $12 more than she earned last weekend. If she earned $48 this weekend, which equation could be used to find out how much she earned last weekend (*b*)?
- Ⓐ $b + 6 = 48$
- Ⓑ $b + 12 = 48$
- Ⓒ $\frac{48}{b} = 12$
- Ⓓ $12b = 48$

74 Mario went to the store to buy a CD player at a regular price of $129. When he got to the store, he saw that it was on sale for 30% off the regular price. How much did Mario pay for the CD player?
- Ⓕ $38.70
- Ⓖ $90.30
- Ⓗ $99.00
- Ⓙ $125.13

75 Which figure does NOT have turn symmetry?

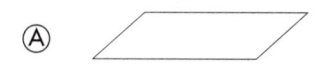

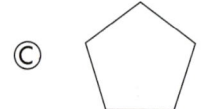

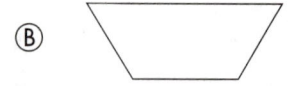

- Ⓐ
- Ⓑ
- Ⓒ
- Ⓓ

106

Advantage Test Prep Grade 6 © 2004 Creative Teaching Press

76 The sixth-grade class is taking a trip to the city by bus. Each bus can hold 56 people. How many buses will they need if there are 135 students and 10 teachers and parents going on the trip?
- F 2
- G 3
- H 4
- J 5

77 What is the value of $2^3 + 3^2$?
- A 15
- B 17
- C 72
- D 3,125

78 Which equation does NOT have a solution of 6?
- F $6p = 36$
- G $q + 9 = 15$
- H $r - 5 = 1$
- J $s/5 = 30$

79 Mindy read $1/3$ of a book on Monday, $1/5$ of it on Tuesday, and $1/6$ of it on Wednesday. What part of the book does she still have to read?
- A $1/3$
- B $3/10$
- C $7/10$
- D $11/14$

80 Megan bought a rug that is 8.5 feet long and 4.8 feet wide. What is the area of the rug?
- F 26.6 feet
- G 26.6 square feet
- H 40.8 feet
- J 40.8 square feet

Answer Key

Reading

Page 8

The answer is option J, *the remainder*. The paragraph does not discuss any kind of motion, which rules out options F, G, and H.

Page 9

The answer is F, *cheap*. *Support* and *neglect* are opposites, and so are *expensive* and *cheap*. Option G means the same as *expensive*. Options H and J relate to *expensive*, but they do not mean the opposite.

Page 10

Answers may vary slightly, but they should be similar to this: *We must find ways to use the rain forests without destroying them because they are the source of important medicines.*

Page 11

The answer is G. The passage says that scientists have millions of plants left to test. Although plants are an important source of medicines, the passage does not suggest that they are the most important source (option F). The clearing and cutting of trees and plants suggest that people are destroying these forests and may wipe them out (option H). The passage hints that logging companies, among others, are significant threats to the forests (option J).

Page 12

Option H happens last. The correct order is options G, J, F, H.

Page 13

Possible answers include: *Both kinds of forests are being threatened by farming and logging. Both kinds of forests are beautiful and worth protecting.*

Page 15

The answer is option H. The villagers think Amrita is wise and look to her for guidance. The actions in options F, G, and J all happen in the story, but they do not show that the villagers respect Amrita.

Page 16

Students' answers may vary, but they should support their opinions with logical reasons. Many might say that from now on, the Maharajah will tell his soldiers to be careful not to cut down forests that protect villages because he has seen firsthand the strength of sandstorms.

Page 17

Option H is correct. After the sandstorm, the Maharajah decided not to cut the trees because he could see that they protected the village. Thus, options F and G are incorrect. Option J is incorrect because the Maharajah wanted the trees to build his fortress. He was not just trying to show who was in charge.

Page 18

The answer is option G. The passage does not suggest option F or J. Option H is a fact, but it is not a use of symbolism.

Page 19

Option F is correct. Options G and H do not describe the important events. Option J is a message from the passage, but it does not summarize the events.

Page 21

The poem is written in the first person because it includes the pronouns *I* and *my*.

Page 22

No, the setting could not be changed to a different season, be moved indoors, or take place in a tropical climate where trees don't drop their leaves. The poem must take place outside in the fall someplace where trees drop their leaves.

Page 23

Option H is correct. The fifth stanza says the leaves grew duller from contact with earth. The leaves were already lightweight (option F), and they rustled only when someone moved them (option G). They did not heap into mountains as a result of lying on the ground; they had to be raked into mountains (option J).

Page 24

Option J is correct. It goes beyond the stated meaning, applying the poet's message to life. Who knows the true value of leaves or anything else? Option F does not go beyond the meaning of the words. Frost does not seem concerned about when to stop raking (option G) or how long he should rake (option H).

Page 25

Option G is the answer. The scale gives the distance for 3 miles. By comparing the scale to the distance from Crescent City to the closest edge of the park, you can see that both are about the same length, 3 miles.

Page 26

The annual rings continue from the center of the heartwood to the outside layer of the sapwood.

Page 27

Option F is the answer. The whole graph on the right represents the number of redwoods still standing. The 4% area on the left graph also represents the number of redwoods still standing. Options G, H, and J are incorrect.

Page 28

No, it doesn't. *Infectious* would be listed between *indigenous* and *invertebrate*.

Page 29

Option J is correct. *Deciduous* means falling off seasonally or as part of a life cycle. Many trees (option F), teeth (option G), and leaves (option H) are deciduous, but evergreens do not lose their needles seasonally or as part of a life cycle. They are not deciduous.

Language
Page 40

Option G is correct. In option F, *my* should be capitalized, and the end mark should be a period. In option H, *friend* should not be capitalized, but *white house* should be. In option J, *white house* and *washington* should be capitalized, and the end mark should be a period.

Page 41

Option G is correct. Option F is an indirect quotation and should not have quotation marks. Option H is missing a comma after *school* and after *said*. Option J is also missing the two commas, and it is missing quotation marks after *school* and before *I'll*.

Page 42

The answer is option G, which combines two independent clauses with a semicolon. Option F runs two clauses together with no punctuation. Options H and J combine clauses with a comma but no conjunction.

Page 43

The answer is H. *It's* is the contraction of *It is*. Option F is a possessive pronoun: The dog chased *its* tail. Option G is not a proper word. Option J is a contraction of *It will*, which does not make sense in this sentence.

Page 44

The answer is H. The plural of *ranch* is *ranches*. This word ends in s, so to make it possessive, you just add an apostrophe. Option F is misspelled and is not possessive. Option G is also misspelled. Option J has the apostrophe in the wrong place.

Page 45

The answer is F. The pronoun *They* takes the place of *Mrs. Green and her husband*. Options G, H, and J are all singular.

Page 46

The correct option is H. *Find* is an irregular verb that changes its spelling in the past tense. Options F and G are misspellings. Option J is present tense, not past tense.

Page 47

The answer is J, which is in past tense. *Last night* tells you that this action happened in the past. Options F, G, and H do not make sense in this sentence. Option F suggests that the action happened several times, while option G says it will happen in the future. Option H indicates that it is happening now.

Page 48

Option G is correct. *Salty* is a more specific adjective than options F, H, and J.

Page 49

The answer is H. *Completely* is an adverb that tells *how* Sheila described the map. Options F and G are adjectives. Option J does not make sense because nothing is being compared in this sentence.

Page 50

Option F is correct. This sentence compares only two things (two times of day), and *wise* is a short adjective, so *wiser* is correct. Option G compares more than two things, while option H incorrectly uses *more* with a short adjective. Option J compares more than two things and uses *most* with a short adjective.

Page 51
Option G is correct. Options F, H, and J do not make sense in this sentence.

Page 52
Option F is correct because *lying on the table* follows the word it describes, *folders*. Options G and J suggest that the assistant is lying on the table. Option H is not possible.

Page 53
Option H is correct. The prepositional phrase *to the library* acts as a modifier that tells *where* I go, so it should follow the words *when I go*. This phrase is misplaced in options F, G, and J, confusing the meaning of the sentence.

Page 54
Option G is not a sentence because it does not have a subject. Options F, H, and J are complete sentences.

Page 55
Option F is correct. This spelling means "a tube that carries blood." Option G is a weather vane, while option H means "proud of your appearance." Option J is a misspelling.

Page 56
The answer is J. This term is hyphenated, making options F and G incorrect. Option H is missing one hyphen.

Mathematics
Page 58
Option F is correct. The 2 is in the ten thousands place so its value is 2 x 10,000, or 20,000. The 9 is in the thousands place, so its value is 9 x 1,000, or 9,000. The 6 is in the tens place, so its value is 6 x 10, or 60. The 5 is in the tenths place, so its value is 0.5.

Page 59
Option J is correct. You can change all the numbers to fractions with denominators of 100. $\frac{3}{25} \times \frac{4}{4} = \frac{12}{100}$. 30% = $\frac{30}{100}$, and 0.4 = $\frac{4}{10}$ = $\frac{40}{100}$. The fractions from least to greatest are $\frac{30}{100}$, $\frac{12}{100}$, and $\frac{40}{100}$. So, the numbers in order from least to greatest are 30%, $\frac{3}{25}$, 0.4.

Page 60
Five squared means 5 multiplied by itself 2 times; 5 x 5 = 25. Two to the fifth power means 2 multiplied by itself 5 times; 2 x 2 x 2 x 2 x 2 = 32. Since 25 x 32 = 800, option G is correct.

Page 61
Did you simplify the fraction after finding the difference between $\frac{9}{10}$ and $\frac{2}{5}$? $\frac{9}{10} - \frac{2}{5} = \frac{9}{10} - \frac{4}{10} = \frac{5}{10} = \frac{1}{2}$. Option H is the correct answer.

Page 62
Option F is correct. The sum of two negative integers is a negative integer, so you can eliminate options H and J. When you add two negative integers, you find the sum of the numbers and keep the sign.

Page 63
Option H is the right choice. Did you move the decimal point in both the dividend and divisor two places to the right? Did you add a zero as a placeholder after the last digit in the dividend? The problem becomes 720 ÷ 45 = 16.

Page 64
Did you rewrite $3\frac{1}{3}$ as an improper fraction? Did you remember to multiply by the reciprocal of the divisor $\frac{5}{6}$? Did you change the improper fraction to a mixed number? The correct choice is option J.

Page 65
Did you choose option G? The quotient of two integers with different signs is negative. 56 divided by 4 is 14, so 56 ÷ (-4) = -14.

Page 66
Option H is correct. Options F and G both have a value of 17. Option J has a value of 13.

Page 67
Did you choose option H? Here's how to find compatible numbers to solve this problem: Look at the first digit in each number in the problem. Since the first digit of the divisor is 4, think of the basic facts for 4. Since 4 x 2 = 8, use 8,000 as a compatible number for 7,892 and 40 as a compatible number for 41. 8,000 ÷ 40 = 200.

Page 68

Option F is correct. The factors of 20 are 1, 2, 4, 5, 10, and 20. The factors of 48 are 1, 2, 3, 4, 6, 8, 12, 16, 24, and 48. The GCF is 4. The GCF for 24 and 48 (option G) is 24. The GCF for 8 and 24 (option H) is 8. The GCF for 8 and 48 (option J) is 8.

Page 69

Option G is correct. The multiples of 4 are 4, 8, 12, 16, 20, 24, 28, 32, 36, 40, . . . The multiples of 9 are 9, 18, 36, . . . The LCM is 36. The LCM for 6 and 18 (option F) is 18. The LCM for 3 and 12 (option H) is 12. The LCM for 2 and 18 (option J) is 18.

Page 70

Did you choose option H? The value of 2^2 is 4. The value of 5^2 is 25. 4 x 25 =100.

Page 71

Did you choose option G? This problem is easier to solve if you substitute each radius choice into the circumference formula. Since each radius choice is a multiple of 7, use $22/7$ for π. Using the formula C = 2πr, C = 2 x $22/7$ x 14 = 88. For option F, the circumference is 44 inches. For option H, the circumference is 132 inches. For option J, the circumference is 176 inches.

Page 72

Since you are classifying the triangle by the lengths of its sides, you can eliminate option J. Since two of the sides have the same length, the triangle must be *isosceles.* The correct answer is option H.

Page 73

The correct answer is option F because the sum of the measures of the angles is 190°. The sum of the measures of the angles for options G, H, and J is 180°.

Page 74

The correct answer is option J. Since 1 foot = 12 inches, to find the number of inches in 6 feet you would multiply 6 x 12, which is 72.

Page 75

Did you choose option H? Since angle C is an obtuse angle, you can eliminate options G and J, which are acute angles. Since similar figures have the same shape, the angle that is congruent to angle C is angle Y.

Page 76

Option F is correct. To find the value of the expression, you substitute the given value for *n* in the given expression. You must remember to use the order of operations. $3n + 4$ = 3 x 2 + 4 = 6 + 4 = 10.

Page 77

Option J is correct. The solutions for options F, G, and H are all $y = 15$. To solve the equation in option F, divide both sides of the equation by 3. To solve the equation in option G, add 7 to both sides of the equation. To solve the equation in option H, multiply both sides of the equation by 5. The solution for option J is $y = 3$. You get this solution by subtracting 6 from both sides of the equation.

Page 78

Option J is correct. Don't be fooled by extra information. You do not need to know that Emilio has saved $150. To find how much Emilio will pay for the television set, first find the amount of the sales tax. Since 6% can be written as the decimal 0.06, multiply $179 x 0.06 to find the amount of the sales tax. $179 x 0.06 = $10.74. Add $179 + $10.74 to find out how much he will pay. $179 + $10.74 = $189.74.

Page 79

Option J is correct. Since the problem is asking for an estimate, you do not need an exact answer. First, you need to estimate the area of Paul's bedroom. Round 11 feet to 10 feet and 14 feet to 15 feet and find the product. The area of the bedroom is about 150 square feet. Then by multiplying 150 by $3, you get an estimate of $450 for the total cost of the tile.

Page 80

Option G is the right choice. The letters A, T, and W all have line symmetry, but the letter S does not.

Practice Test: Reading

1. B
2. J
3. Students should conclude that the new food pyramid will have more categories to indicate that we should eat less saturated fats and more polyunsaturated fats and less refined carbohydrates and more complex carbohydrates.
4. F
5. C
6. G
7. C
8. H
9. B
10. H
11. B
12. Answers will vary, but students might suggest that Megan will look for Haley and try to become her friend.
13. C
14. F
15. C
16. Answers may vary, but students should recognize that the shelter location is more important to the story than the time period, which is probably present time.
17. B
18. Students should point out that the two characters are the same sex and about the same age. They are also both willing to help others. However, Megan lives in a house, and Haley seems to be homeless.
19. C
20. F

Practice Test: Language

21. D
22. G
23. C
24. H
25. D
26. H
27. A
28. G
29. C
30. G
31. A
32. H
33. D
34. J
35. B
36. H
37. D
38. G
39. C
40. F
41. C
42. J
43. C
44. H
45. C
46. F
47. A
48. G
49. A
50. J

Practice Test: Math

51. C
52. J
53. B
54. H
55. C
56. F
57. B
58. H
59. C
60. F
61. B
62. F
63. A
64. G
65. C
66. G
67. D
68. G
69. D
70. H
71. D
72. J
73. B
74. G
75. B
76. G
77. B
78. J
79. G
80. J